All About Andes Mountains: A Kid's Guide to the Longest Mountain Range

Educational Books For Kids, Volume 47

Shah Rukh

Published by Shah Rukh, 2024.

While every precaution has been taken in the preparation of this book, the publisher assumes no responsibility for errors or omissions, or for damages resulting from the use of the information contained herein.

ALL ABOUT ANDES MOUNTAINS: A KID'S GUIDE TO THE LONGEST MOUNTAIN RANGE

First edition. November 9, 2024.

Written by Shah Rukh.

Table of Contents

Prologue

Welcome to the Andes Mountains! Stretching over 4,300 miles along the western edge of South America, the Andes are more than just mountains—they're a world of adventure, history, and mystery waiting to be discovered. From ancient civilizations and mighty volcanoes to rare animals and hidden treasures, the Andes Mountains have captured the imagination of explorers and adventurers for thousands of years.

Imagine a place where giant peaks reach up into the clouds, where snow-capped summits tower over lush rainforests, and where winding rivers carve their way through deep valleys. The Andes are home to amazing animals like the graceful llama, the soaring Andean condor, and the elusive jaguar. This mountain range has some of the world's highest volcanoes, ancient ruins like Machu Picchu, and vibrant cultures that have called these mountains home for generations.

But life in the Andes isn't always easy. People have had to adapt to high altitudes, where the air is thin, the weather is harsh, and survival requires bravery and creativity. Over the centuries, the people of the Andes developed ways to live off the land, grow food on steep mountainsides, and protect their traditions and stories.

In this book, you'll discover the wonders of the Andes, learn about the creatures, plants, and people who make this place so special, and explore the science and secrets hidden in these ancient peaks. So, grab your imagination and get ready for a journey through the longest mountain range in the world—the Andes Mountains await!

Chapter 1: Discovering the Andes Mountains

Imagine a mountain range so long it stretches through seven countries, covering almost the entire west side of South America. This is the Andes Mountains, the longest mountain range in the world! The Andes are like a giant backbone for South America, winding through Venezuela, Colombia, Ecuador, Peru, Bolivia, Chile, and Argentina. It stretches for over 4,300 miles (7,000 kilometers), almost like going from one end of the United States to the other, twice! If you looked at a map of South America, you'd see the Andes running all the way from the top to the bottom of the continent, towering over jungles, deserts, valleys, and even some cities.

The Andes are not just one line of mountains but a collection of many ranges, which is like having several long, tall rows of mountains stacked side by side. Some of these peaks are extremely high. In fact, the highest peak, Mount Aconcagua in Argentina, reaches about 22,841 feet (6,961 meters) above sea level! That's taller than any other mountain outside of Asia. And throughout the Andes, there are dozens of other peaks that rise above 20,000 feet (6,100 meters), so they're often covered in snow, even though they're located near the Equator, where it's typically warm. Because the Andes are so tall, they affect the climate around them in powerful ways. Some parts of the Andes have icy glaciers, while others have dry, sandy deserts nearby!

The Andes have been forming for millions of years. They were created by tectonic plates, the massive pieces of the Earth's crust that slowly shift and move. When two plates—specifically the Nazca Plate and the South American Plate—started pressing against each other, they crumpled up, creating the Andes Mountains. This process is still happening, so the Andes are growing bit by bit each year! Sometimes, this movement causes earthquakes in the region, as the plates push and shove beneath the mountains. Because they're still growing and changing, scientists find the Andes especially interesting to study.

The Andes Mountains are full of surprises! Alongside towering peaks, you'll find volcanoes—both active and dormant. Some of these volcanoes erupt every now and then, and scientists keep a close watch on them to predict any changes that might signal an eruption. The Andes also have something called plateaus, which are large, flat areas high up in the mountains. One famous plateau is the Altiplano, shared by Bolivia and Peru, where some people live and grow crops despite the high altitude. And nestled among the high peaks and rugged cliffs, you'll even find lakes. Lake Titicaca, the largest lake in South America, sits at an altitude of over 12,000 feet (3,658 meters) and is one of the highest navigable lakes in the world!

The Andes aren't just famous for their natural wonders; they're also rich in history and culture. Long ago, the Inca Empire, one of the greatest ancient civilizations of South America, made its home in these mountains. The Inca people built an extensive network of roads across the Andes, connecting their empire and helping them travel, trade, and communicate. They used stones to construct incredible buildings, like the famous city of Machu Picchu in Peru, which is still standing today, even after centuries. The Andes provided the Incas with everything they needed, from fertile lands for farming to rivers full of fish. They even built terraces, or giant steps, on the slopes to grow potatoes, corn, and other crops, making the most of every bit of land. Today, many people still live in the Andes, and some of their customs and traditions come from the time of the Incas, making the mountains a place where ancient history and modern life come together.

The Andes have a vast variety of plants and animals, many of which are unique and can't be found anywhere else. You might spot the llama, a furry animal that has been used by people in the Andes for transportation and wool for hundreds of years. There are also alpacas, which are similar to llamas but smaller, with incredibly soft wool that's used to make warm clothing. In the forests of the Andes, you might find colorful birds, such as the Andean condor, which has one of the largest wingspans of any bird, reaching up to 10 feet (3 meters)! The condor is an important symbol in the Andes and appears in many local stories and legends. High up in the Andes, some plants and animals have to adapt to the cold temperatures and low oxygen levels. There are plants like the puya raimondii, which can grow over 30 feet (9 meters) tall and bloom only once in its long lifetime, then die.

Because the Andes span such a long distance, different parts of the range have very different climates. In the northern Andes, near Venezuela and Colombia, it's warmer and wetter, with lush forests and plenty of rain. As you travel south toward Peru and Bolivia, the mountains become drier, and there's more high-altitude desert. Near Chile and Argentina in the southern Andes, the weather becomes colder, with icy winds and snow covering the peaks during much of the year. This variety in climate means the Andes are home to many types of ecosystems, each with its own plants and animals. In some parts, you'll find tropical rainforests with dense, green vegetation and monkeys swinging from trees. In other parts, like the Atacama Desert in Chile, it almost never rains, and the landscape is rocky and barren.

The Andes Mountains have a strong influence on the people who live there. Many villages are located high up on the mountain slopes, where people have learned to adapt to the challenging environment. Because it can be tough to breathe at such high altitudes, the people who live here have larger lungs and more red blood cells to help them get enough oxygen. Many people in the Andes practice traditional ways of life, farming crops like potatoes, quinoa, and corn, just as their ancestors did. They also raise llamas and alpacas, whose wool is used to make warm, colorful clothing, often woven in beautiful patterns that represent the culture and stories of their communities.

Throughout the Andes, there are many celebrations, festivals, and traditions that honor the mountains, nature, and ancestors. Some of these traditions go back thousands of years, blending Inca beliefs with Christian influences brought by Spanish explorers. Festivals are times for communities to come together, dress in bright clothes, play music, dance, and share food. Many festivals are connected to the agricultural cycle, celebrating the harvest or asking for a good growing season. For people in the Andes, the mountains aren't just a place to live; they're also a source of inspiration, a protector, and a sacred space filled with stories and legends passed down through generations.

The Andes Mountains are not only a natural wonder; they're a living, breathing part of history, culture, and life. They continue to amaze people with their beauty, their power, and their mysteries, drawing adventurers, scientists, and travelers from around the world who come to explore their peaks, study their ecosystems, and learn about the cultures that call them home. The Andes truly stand as a grand and majestic presence, reaching toward the sky and holding countless secrets among their towering peaks and deep valleys.

Chapter 2: Secrets of the Ancient Incas

The Incas were one of the most incredible civilizations in history, with a culture full of mysteries, achievements, and secrets that continue to fascinate people today. They lived in South America, mainly in the Andes Mountains, around 600 years ago, creating a massive empire called Tawantinsuyu. This name means "Land of the Four Regions" in their language, Quechua. Their empire was so large that it covered parts of present-day Peru, Ecuador, Bolivia, Chile, Argentina, and Colombia. Despite having no written language like we do today, the Incas managed to organize and control one of the largest and most powerful empires ever seen in the Americas, filled with incredible buildings, roads, and a rich culture.

One of the greatest mysteries about the Incas is how they built their empire without the use of wheels or iron tools. The Inca people built amazing structures using only simple tools made from stone, bronze, and wood. They didn't have steel or iron, yet they created strong and beautiful cities high up in the mountains, like Machu Picchu, the famous "Lost City of the Incas." Machu Picchu is one of the best-preserved examples of Inca architecture. Its buildings are made from large, perfectly cut stones that fit together so tightly that even a knife blade can't fit between them. The Incas didn't use any mortar (a kind of glue for stones) to hold the rocks together, yet their buildings have withstood earthquakes and storms for centuries.

Another fascinating secret of the Incas was their ability to create terraces for farming on steep mountain slopes. Since the Andes are mostly high mountains, flat farmland was hard to find. The Incas solved this problem by creating terraces—steps carved into the mountainside. These terraces helped prevent soil from washing away, allowed them to grow crops at different heights for different climates, and provided enough food to feed the entire empire. The Incas grew many kinds of crops, such as potatoes, corn, quinoa, and beans, which were vital to their diet. They even had ways to store food for long periods, which helped them survive droughts or times when crops didn't grow well. Their knowledge of agriculture was advanced, and their techniques are still used by people living in the Andes today.

The Incas had a unique way of recording information. They didn't have a written language like we do, but they used something called a "quipu." A quipu was a collection of colored strings with knots tied in different places. The colors, number of strings, and the types of knots all represented different pieces of information. This system helped the Incas keep records of important things, like the amount of crops harvested, the population in each area, and supplies needed for the army. It was a very organized and detailed way of keeping track of things, even though it might look simple to us. Scientists and historians are still trying to fully understand how quipus worked, and some secrets of the quipu system remain unsolved.

Communication across their vast empire was another incredible achievement. The Incas built thousands of miles of roads that connected different parts of their empire, from the deserts near the coast to the high peaks of the Andes. These roads were used by messengers called "chasquis," who ran in relay teams to deliver messages and goods quickly across the empire. Chasquis were highly trained runners, and they could run long distances at high altitudes. They carried messages, quipus, and even small items in a pouch. Each chasqui would run to a "tambo," a rest station where they would pass the message or item to the next runner. In this way, information could travel incredibly fast across the empire without the need for horses or wheels.

Religion played a huge role in Inca society, and they believed in many gods, each with a different power and purpose. The most important god was Inti, the sun god. The Incas believed that their emperor, or "Sapa Inca," was a descendant of Inti and that he had divine power. To honor Inti, the Incas built grand temples, like the

Coricancha in Cusco, which was covered in gold to reflect the sun's rays. Gold held a special meaning for the Incas, as they believed it was the sweat of the sun. The Incas also worshiped other gods, like Pachamama, the earth goddess, and Mama Cocha, the goddess of the sea. Their religious ceremonies often included offerings of food, textiles, and sometimes even animals. They believed that by making these offerings, they could maintain balance in the world and ensure good harvests and protection from natural disasters.

The Incas also held certain places in the natural world as sacred. Mountains, rivers, lakes, and large rocks were seen as "huacas," or sacred places, where spirits were believed to dwell. Many of these places were chosen as sites for temples or important ceremonies, as the Incas believed that these locations held special energy. One example is the Sacred Valley in Peru, where the Incas built temples and farms and held festivals to honor the gods. Even the city of Cusco, the capital of the Inca Empire, was designed to be shaped like a puma, a sacred animal symbolizing strength. The Incas believed that by aligning their cities and temples with nature, they could create harmony and show respect for their gods.

The Incas were skilled in astronomy, which is the study of stars and planets. They watched the movements of the sun, moon, and stars closely and used their observations to plan their farming and religious festivals. They built special pillars called "intihuatana," which means "hitching post of the sun," to track the sun's position during different times of the year. These pillars helped the Incas know when to plant and harvest crops and when to celebrate important events. They also believed that constellations in the night sky represented animals and spirits. The Incas saw the Milky Way, a bright band of stars, as a celestial river and believed that certain animals, like the llama, lived in the sky.

One of the most well-known mysteries of the Inca culture is the sudden decline of their empire. When Spanish explorers arrived in the early 1500s, they found the Inca Empire at the height of its power, but only a few decades later, it had collapsed. There were many reasons for this downfall. The Spanish brought with them diseases, such as smallpox, which spread quickly among the Inca people, who had never been exposed to these illnesses before. This led to a significant loss of life. Additionally, the Spanish had advanced weapons and horses, which gave them an advantage in battles. The Spanish also made alliances with other native groups who were unhappy with Inca rule, which weakened the empire from within.

Despite the fall of the Inca Empire, the legacy of the Incas lives on today. Many descendants of the Incas still live in the Andes Mountains, carrying on traditional ways of farming, weaving, and celebrating festivals. Some people still speak Quechua, the language of the Incas, and continue to honor the ancient gods, like Inti and Pachamama, in their ceremonies. Inca traditions, crafts, and music are still important parts of life in the Andes, keeping the spirit of the ancient empire alive. The ancient buildings, roads, and terraces left behind by the Incas continue to stand as a reminder of their incredible achievements and the mysteries that remain unsolved.

The Incas remain a fascinating civilization because they achieved so much with limited technology, and many questions about their lives, beliefs, and culture still puzzle historians. Even today, archaeologists uncover new artifacts and pieces of information that add to our understanding of the Incas. Whether it's the mystery of the quipus, the engineering marvel of Machu Picchu, or the story of their resilient culture, the Incas' secrets continue to inspire people around the world to learn more about this incredible civilization.

Chapter 3: Exploring Cloud Forests and Valleys

Cloud forests and valleys are two of the most magical and mysterious places found in the Andes Mountains. High up in the mountains, where the air is cool and damp, cloud forests thrive. Imagine a forest so misty that it feels like walking through clouds – that's why they're called cloud forests. These forests are often covered in fog and mist, especially in the mornings, which gives them a magical and mysterious appearance. The cloud forest is a special place because of its unique climate, which is both warm and humid but also cool, thanks to its high altitude. These special conditions create the perfect home for all kinds of plants and animals that can't be found anywhere else in the world.

One of the amazing things about cloud forests is the huge variety of plants that grow there. Many plants in the cloud forest look different from the ones we're used to seeing. There are towering trees with thick branches, and their bark is often covered with moss, ferns, and even orchids that cling to the trees like colorful decorations. This is because the air is always moist, so plants can grow on top of each other. Some plants, called epiphytes, don't even need soil to grow! They attach themselves to the branches and trunks of other plants to soak up moisture from the mist and gather nutrients from the air. Some of these epiphytes, like bromeliads, even collect water in their leaves, creating tiny pools where frogs and insects live.

The animals of the cloud forest are as unique as the plants. Because the cloud forests are so high up, the animals that live here have adapted to the cool temperatures and wet climate. You might see brightly colored birds, like the Andean cock-of-the-rock, with its fiery red feathers and strange fan-shaped crest. There's also the spectacled bear, the only bear species in South America, which is known for the light-colored markings around its eyes that look like glasses. These bears are very shy and mostly eat plants, especially the tender parts of bromeliads. The cloud forest is also home to monkeys, hummingbirds, butterflies, and countless insects, each adapted to life in this damp, green world. High up in the trees, tiny frogs live in the water-filled leaves of bromeliads, and some of these frogs are brilliantly colored, warning other animals that they are poisonous.

Cloud forests also have some amazing creatures that are very good at hiding. Many animals here are nocturnal, which means they come out only at night when it's dark. This helps them avoid predators. For example, some species of owls and bats fly through the misty forest after sunset, hunting for insects and small animals. Some insects, like stick insects, have developed camouflage, which means they look like sticks or leaves, making it very hard to see them. The cloud forests are like a hidden world full of surprises, and every leaf, branch, and shadow might be hiding something new to discover.

Cloud forests are important not only because they are beautiful but also because they play a vital role in the environment. These forests are like giant sponges. They catch moisture from the clouds and store it in the plants, soil, and moss. When it rains or when the clouds are especially thick, the forest absorbs the water, and this water slowly seeps down into the ground. This process helps keep rivers and streams flowing, even during dry seasons, which is important for the people, plants, and animals that live downstream. The trees and plants also help to prevent soil erosion, which means they stop the soil from washing away during heavy rains, keeping the land stable.

But cloud forests aren't the only amazing parts of the Andes. In the valleys below, a different world exists with its own plants, animals, and climate. Valleys are the lower areas between mountains, and in the Andes, they are often long, wide, and filled with lush vegetation. Many valleys have rivers running through them, bringing life to the land. The rivers start high up in the mountains, where snow and glaciers melt, and flow down through the valleys, creating fertile soil that's perfect for farming. The valleys in the Andes are often warmer than the cloud forests above, which allows for different kinds of plants to grow. You'll find crops like potatoes, corn, and quinoa being grown by farmers, just as they have for thousands of years.

The valleys of the Andes are also home to a variety of animals, some of which are different from those in the cloud forest. For example, in the warmer valleys, you might see llamas and alpacas grazing on the hillsides. These animals have been domesticated by people living in the Andes for centuries and are used for their wool, meat, and as pack animals to carry goods across the rugged mountain terrain. The Andean condor, one of the world's largest flying birds, also glides through the valleys, using the warm air currents to soar high above the ground in search of food. Watching a condor in flight is an amazing sight – with wings that can span over 10 feet, they are graceful and powerful, almost like a symbol of the Andes themselves.

The rivers that flow through the valleys are essential to life in the Andes. Not only do they provide water for crops and drinking, but they also create small microclimates, or pockets of unique weather. Near rivers, you might find dense patches of vegetation with fruit trees and flowering plants that attract bees, butterflies, and birds. These river valleys are often the sites of small towns and villages, where people have built communities and farms. People living in these valleys have a strong connection to the land and rely on it for their daily lives. Many still practice traditional farming techniques, using terraces to grow crops on the steep valley sides, just like their Inca ancestors did.

Both cloud forests and valleys have a rich cultural importance. For thousands of years, the people of the Andes have lived in harmony with these landscapes, treating them with respect. The forests and valleys are seen as sacred places, filled with spirits and gods that protect the land and the people. Ancient traditions and ceremonies are still held to honor the natural world, asking for blessings on the harvest or protection from natural disasters. The native people have a deep understanding of the plants and animals, knowing which plants can be used as medicine, which animals are friendly or dangerous, and how to predict the weather by watching the clouds, birds, and other signs from nature.

One challenge facing the cloud forests and valleys today is climate change. As temperatures rise and weather patterns change, the delicate balance of these ecosystems is at risk. For example, some cloud forests are becoming warmer and drier, which makes it harder for certain plants and animals to survive. Rivers in the valleys may dry up during certain times of the year, affecting both the people and wildlife that rely on them. Conservation efforts are being made to protect these unique ecosystems. Scientists are studying cloud forests and valleys to learn more about how they work, and local communities are working to preserve their traditional ways of life while also protecting the land. Many organizations are working to create protected areas, where the plants, animals, and cultures of the Andes can continue to thrive.

Exploring the cloud forests and valleys of the Andes is like stepping into a different world, where nature, history, and culture are woven together in an incredible way. These landscapes are full of life, from the smallest insects to the towering trees and the majestic Andean condor. Each part of the forest and valley has its own role, and all these elements depend on one another to keep the ecosystem healthy. The cloud forests and valleys are not only home to many amazing species, but they also hold the wisdom of ancient cultures, secrets of nature, and lessons for the future about the importance of taking care of our planet.

Chapter 4: Wildlife Wonders of the Andes

The Andes Mountains are home to some of the most unique and fascinating wildlife in the world. Stretching thousands of miles along the western edge of South America, the Andes create a wide range of habitats that allow for an incredible variety of plants and animals to thrive. The mountains go from tropical rainforests to freezing glaciers, with everything in between. This mix of climates and landscapes means that the Andes are filled with species that have adapted in remarkable ways to survive in high altitudes, extreme temperatures, and dense forests. Some of these animals are found nowhere else on Earth, making the Andes a truly special place for wildlife.

One of the most well-known animals of the Andes is the llama. Llamas are large, gentle animals with long necks and soft, woolly fur that keeps them warm in the chilly mountain air. They have been domesticated, which means people started raising and taking care of them a long time ago, probably thousands of years. The people of the Andes have relied on llamas for generations, using them as pack animals to carry goods over the mountains, as well as for their wool, which is used to make clothing, and even for food. Llamas are strong and can carry heavy loads across the steep, rocky paths of the Andes, which makes them perfect companions for people who live in such rugged terrain. They are also famous for their habit of spitting, which they do to defend themselves or show they are annoyed.

Similar to llamas, alpacas are another type of Andean animal known for their thick, soft fur. Alpacas are smaller than llamas, with a fluffier coat, and they're mainly raised for their wool, which is softer and warmer than sheep's wool. Alpaca wool is highly valued and used to make luxurious blankets, scarves, and sweaters that keep people warm in the cold mountain weather. Alpacas are gentle creatures that graze peacefully on grasses high up in the mountains. They live in herds and have a strong sense of community, huddling together for warmth on cold nights.

Another fascinating Andean animal is the vicuña, a wild relative of the llama and alpaca. Vicuñas are smaller, with delicate features and a sleek body. They have some of the softest fur in the world, which makes their wool very valuable. However, unlike alpacas and llamas, vicuñas are wild and cannot be easily tamed. The ancient Incas valued vicuñas highly and only allowed royalty to wear clothing made from vicuña wool. Today, vicuñas are protected animals, and their wool can only be collected during special gatherings where they are carefully herded, shorn, and then released back into the wild.

High above the mountains soars the Andean condor, one of the largest flying birds in the world. Andean condors have a wingspan that can reach up to 10 feet, which allows them to glide effortlessly over the mountains. They are a type of vulture, meaning they feed mostly on carrion, or dead animals, which helps keep the environment clean by getting rid of decaying bodies. Andean condors are majestic and graceful in the air, riding warm air currents for hours without flapping their wings. Because of their size and power, condors are seen as symbols of strength and freedom in many Andean cultures. They play an important role in local myths and stories, often seen as messengers between the Earth and the heavens.

In the dense cloud forests of the Andes, where mist hangs heavy in the air, lives the spectacled bear. Also known as the Andean bear, it is the only bear species native to South America. Spectacled bears are named for the white markings around their eyes that look like glasses or "spectacles." These bears are mainly vegetarian, feeding on fruits, plants, and even bromeliads, a type of plant that grows on trees in the cloud forest. They are shy and elusive animals, often hiding in the forest, and rarely seen by people. Spectacled bears are skilled climbers, and they sometimes make nests in trees to rest. Although they are gentle, spectacled bears are endangered due to habitat loss as more forests are cleared for farming and development.

The Andes are also home to many colorful birds. One of the most striking is the Andean cock-of-the-rock, known for its bright red feathers and unique fan-shaped crest. Male cocks-of-the-rock have a vivid red-orange color, while females are more brownish, which helps them blend into their surroundings. These birds are famous for their courtship displays, where the males gather in groups to show off their feathers, dance, and make strange clucking sounds to attract females. This behavior, called a "lek," is an important part of their mating ritual. The Andean cock-of-the-rock lives in the cloud forests and is difficult to spot because it tends to stay hidden among dense vegetation. Spotting one in the wild is like discovering a hidden treasure.

Another amazing bird of the Andes is the hummingbird. There are many different species of hummingbirds in the Andes, each with its own beautiful colors and patterns. Some hummingbirds in the Andes have adapted to the cold by growing more feathers and have special muscles that help them stay warm. They are expert flyers, hovering in place to drink nectar from flowers with their long, thin beaks. Hummingbirds are important pollinators, meaning they help plants produce seeds by moving pollen from one flower to another. In the Andes, some flowers have evolved to match the shapes of specific hummingbirds' beaks, creating a special partnership between bird and flower.

Amphibians like frogs are also well-represented in the Andes, especially in the moist cloud forests. Some of these frogs are brightly colored and tiny, and they live in water-filled plants high in the trees. The Andean marsupial frog is particularly fascinating because it has a special way of raising its young. The female carries her eggs in a pouch, similar to how a kangaroo carries its babies. When the eggs hatch, tiny tadpoles emerge and eventually grow into little frogs, all while safely carried by their mother.

In the drier parts of the Andes, like the high-altitude plateaus known as "páramos," you'll find animals adapted to the cold and thin air. Here lives the Andean fox, a clever predator that survives by hunting small animals and scavenging. Andean foxes have thick fur that helps them stay warm, and their diet includes everything from insects to berries to small mammals. The Andean fox is a skilled hunter and is known for its cunning, often sneaking around in search of food. In the same high-altitude regions, you can also find chinchillas, small rodents with soft, dense fur. Chinchillas are adapted to survive in harsh, rocky landscapes, where they hide from predators in crevices and feed on grasses and plants. Because of their luxurious fur, chinchillas have been hunted in the past, and today they are considered a vulnerable species.

Some reptiles, like the Andean iguana, have also adapted to survive in the cooler temperatures of the Andes. These lizards are found in rocky areas where they can bask in the sun to warm up. Andean iguanas have unique colors that help them blend into their surroundings, which protects them from predators. Although reptiles are not as common in the Andes as they are in warmer, lower areas, a few species have managed to make this high-altitude environment their home.

The rivers and lakes in the Andes are filled with unique aquatic life as well. One of the most famous fish is the Andean catfish, which lives in the cold, clear mountain streams. Andean rivers are also home to many freshwater crabs, small fish, and insects that provide food for birds and mammals. In some high-altitude lakes, there are even freshwater shrimp and other small creatures adapted to the cold, low-oxygen water.

The wildlife of the Andes isn't just interesting to look at; it also plays a crucial role in the health of the entire ecosystem. Each animal, from the smallest insect to the largest condor, is connected in a web of relationships. Some animals, like hummingbirds and bees, help pollinate plants, which allows those plants to produce fruit and seeds. Other animals, like the Andean condor, act as nature's cleaners, feeding on dead animals and helping prevent the spread of disease. The grazing of animals like llamas and alpacas keeps the grasslands healthy, while predators like foxes help control the populations of smaller animals.

Unfortunately, many animals of the Andes are facing threats due to human activities. Deforestation, mining, and climate change are affecting the delicate balance of the Andean ecosystems. As people clear more land for farming and development, animals lose their habitats and have to move to new areas, which can be dangerous and challenging for them. Conservation efforts are underway to protect these unique animals and their habitats. National parks and wildlife reserves have been established to provide safe spaces for Andean wildlife, and local communities are working to preserve traditional ways of living that respect the environment.

The animals of the Andes are a true wonder, adapted to survive in one of the most challenging and varied environments on Earth. From the gentle llama to the soaring condor, each animal has a role to play in the high-altitude ecosystems of the Andes. Exploring the wildlife wonders of the Andes is like discovering a world within a world – a place where nature has created new forms and new ways of living, allowing life to thrive in the thin mountain air and misty forests. As more people learn about these amazing creatures, there is hope that the Andes and its wildlife will continue to be protected for future generations to enjoy and learn from.

Chapter 5: Mighty Peaks and Tall Summits

The Andes Mountains are known for their dramatic and towering peaks, some of the tallest and most majestic in the world. Stretching over 4,300 miles along the western edge of South America, the Andes are not just one mountain range but a series of ranges that include rugged peaks, deep valleys, and high plateaus. This great chain of mountains includes some of the highest summits outside of Asia. These mighty peaks are not only breathtaking to look at but are also rich with history, ancient legends, and incredible ecosystems. Each peak has its own story, and many of them have played important roles in the cultures and lives of the people who live in the Andes.

One of the most famous and tallest peaks in the Andes is Mount Aconcagua. Located in Argentina near the Chilean border, Aconcagua stands at an impressive 22,841 feet, making it the highest mountain in both the Andes and the entire Western Hemisphere. Climbing Aconcagua is no easy feat. With its extreme heights and cold temperatures, it attracts adventurers and climbers from all over the world who want to reach its snowy summit. Although it does not require as much technical climbing as some other high peaks, Aconcagua presents many challenges due to its thin air and unpredictable weather. Reaching the top means pushing through high winds, freezing temperatures, and the possibility of altitude sickness, which happens when people's bodies struggle to get enough oxygen at such high elevations. Those who do make it to the top are rewarded with a stunning view that stretches across the Andes, as well as a sense of accomplishment for conquering one of the mightiest peaks on Earth.

Another significant peak in the Andes is Mount Chimborazo in Ecuador. Chimborazo is especially interesting because, although it is not the highest peak in the Andes (it stands at about 20,549 feet), it is actually the farthest point from the center of the Earth. This is because the Earth is not a perfect sphere; it bulges slightly at the equator, making mountains near the equator farther from the center of the planet than even Mount Everest. Chimborazo's summit is covered in glaciers that sparkle in the sunlight, and it has long been a place of mystery and respect for the native people of Ecuador. In ancient times, local tribes would make offerings to the mountain, treating it as a powerful spirit or god that could bring good fortune or disaster. Today, Chimborazo remains a symbol of natural wonder and is a popular climbing destination, even though its glaciers are slowly melting due to climate change.

Peru is home to several towering peaks, including Mount Huascarán, the highest mountain in the country at 22,205 feet. Huascarán is located in the Cordillera Blanca, a part of the Andes famous for its snow-covered peaks and scenic beauty. The mountain was named after an Inca emperor, and it is still deeply connected to local traditions and legends. Huascarán's glaciers provide important water sources for the surrounding communities, especially during dry seasons. However, these glaciers are shrinking due to global warming, which worries the people who rely on the mountain's meltwater. Climbing Huascarán is a difficult challenge because of the steep icy slopes, crevasses (deep cracks in the ice), and the risk of avalanches. The Cordillera Blanca is known as a paradise for mountain climbers, with many other peaks over 20,000 feet, and its beautiful scenery attracts thousands of visitors every year.

Further south in Peru lies the awe-inspiring Mount Ausangate. Standing at around 20,945 feet, Ausangate is not just known for its height but also for its colorful slopes. The mountain is covered with stripes of red, orange, turquoise, and gold, created by different minerals in the rocks. This colorful part of the Andes is sometimes called Rainbow Mountain, and it has become a popular attraction for people who want to see its unusual beauty. Ausangate has been sacred to the Quechua people, the descendants of the Inca, for centuries. Every year, thousands of people take part in the Qoyllur Rit'i festival, a pilgrimage that brings them close to the mountain to celebrate and honor it. Ausangate is not only a spiritual place but also a symbol of nature's beauty and diversity, showing how the Andes can surprise and amaze with unexpected colors and formations.

The Andes are also home to the dramatic peaks of the Cordillera Real in Bolivia. One of the most famous peaks here is Illimani, which rises to about 21,122 feet and is visible from the capital city, La Paz. Illimani has four main summits and is often covered in snow, making it a striking sight against the skyline. It is sometimes called "The Sleeping Giant," as its shape looks like a giant resting on its back. For the people of La Paz, Illimani is a protective figure, watching over the city. The mountain is a popular climbing destination, but it is challenging, with steep ice walls and deep snow. Many people in Bolivia see Illimani as more than just a mountain – it's a powerful symbol of the land, the sky, and the spirits that are believed to live in the peaks.

In Chile, you can find Ojos del Salado, the highest active volcano in the world. Ojos del Salado stands at an incredible 22,615 feet, making it the second-highest mountain in the Andes after Aconcagua. Located on the border between Chile and Argentina, this volcano is an impressive sight, with lava formations and snowy slopes. Although it is an active volcano, Ojos del Salado last erupted thousands of years ago, so climbers don't need to worry about eruptions. However, the climb is still difficult because of the high altitude and the harsh, dry desert climate that surrounds it. The mountain is located in the Atacama Desert, one of the driest places on Earth. Climbing to the top of Ojos del Salado means crossing barren, rocky landscapes where there is almost no water. Reaching the summit is a huge achievement for mountaineers and a reminder of the power and mystery of nature.

In Colombia, the Andes split into three smaller ranges known as the Cordillera Occidental, Cordillera Central, and Cordillera Oriental. One of the tallest peaks in Colombia is Nevado del Ruiz, a volcano that reaches 17,457 feet. Nevado del Ruiz is famous not only for its height but also for its volcanic activity. In 1985, it erupted, causing a tragic mudflow that destroyed the town of Armero and took thousands of lives. The eruption was a reminder of the strength and unpredictability of the Andes. Despite its past, Nevado del Ruiz remains an important place for scientific study, with researchers keeping an eye on its activity. This volcano is also important to local indigenous communities, who see it as a place of both power and danger.

Further north, in Venezuela, is Pico Bolívar, the highest mountain in the country at 16,332 feet. Named after Simón Bolívar, the leader who helped South American countries gain independence from Spain, Pico Bolívar is a symbol of national pride. The peak is often covered in snow, though it has become less common due to global warming. Climbing Pico Bolívar is challenging and requires technical skills because of its steep slopes. Unlike the higher peaks in other parts of the Andes, Pico Bolívar's lower altitude makes it more accessible to some climbers, though it is still a difficult climb. For many Venezuelans, Pico Bolívar represents strength, freedom, and the spirit of the Andes.

The Andes also hold countless unnamed or lesser-known peaks, each with its own unique features and beauty. Some of these peaks have jagged, rocky tops, while others are capped with snow and ice. Many of these peaks are difficult to reach, even for the most experienced climbers, and some remain unexplored. The high-altitude environment creates special conditions that can only be found in the Andes, such as glaciers, alpine lakes, and fields of wildflowers that bloom in the short summer season. These places are home to rare animals and plants that have adapted to the cold and harsh conditions. For example, small animals like chinchillas and viscachas (a type of rodent) live among the rocks, while tough mountain plants cling to the slopes, surviving in thin, rocky soil and high winds.

The peaks of the Andes are more than just rocks and ice; they hold a deep cultural and spiritual significance for the indigenous people who have lived in these mountains for thousands of years. Many Andean cultures believe that the mountains are alive, filled with spirits known as "apus," or mountain gods, that watch over the land and its people. These spirits are thought to protect the villages, bring good harvests, and control the weather. People often make offerings, like coca leaves, flowers, or small foods, to show respect to the apus. The mountains are places of worship, reflection, and tradition, connecting the people of the Andes to their history and beliefs.

In modern times, the mighty peaks of the Andes continue to inspire adventurers, scientists, and nature lovers. Climbers come from around the world to test their skills on the high summits, while scientists study the glaciers, rocks, and wildlife to understand more about Earth's history and climate. Photographers and artists capture the beauty of the mountains, sharing it with people who may never get a chance to see the Andes in person. Conservationists work to protect these high-altitude environments, understanding that the mountains are delicate ecosystems that can be easily damaged by human activities and climate change.

The mighty peaks and tall summits of the Andes are places of wonder, challenge, and discovery. They stand as symbols of endurance, power, and natural beauty, rising high into the clouds and offering endless secrets to those who explore them. These towering mountains remind us of the strength of nature and the resilience of the people who live in their shadow. With each peak telling its own story, the Andes Mountains are like a massive, open book of adventures waiting to be read, climbed, and appreciated by people from all around the world.

Chapter 6: Life in the High Altitudes

Living in the high altitudes of the Andes Mountains is a unique and challenging experience. The towering heights, thin air, and extreme temperatures make this region one of the most demanding environments on Earth. Yet, people have been living in these mountainous areas for thousands of years, adapting in fascinating ways to the high altitudes, the rugged terrain, and the often unpredictable weather. The Andean highlands are home to unique cultures, traditions, and lifestyles shaped by the mountains around them, and the people who live there have learned to find strength and resources in places that might seem inhospitable to outsiders.

One of the most important challenges of life in the high Andes is the thin air. At high altitudes, there is less oxygen in the air than at sea level, which can make it harder to breathe. People who visit the Andes from lower altitudes often feel light-headed, dizzy, or tired as their bodies adjust to the lower oxygen levels. This feeling, known as "altitude sickness," can make even simple tasks like walking feel tiring. But the people who have lived in the Andes for generations, known as Andean highlanders, have bodies that have adapted to this environment. Many highlanders have larger lungs, which help them take in more oxygen with each breath, and they have more red blood cells, which are the cells that carry oxygen throughout the body. These natural adaptations allow them to breathe more easily at high altitudes, where the air is thin.

Another important part of life in the high Andes is dealing with extreme temperatures. The Andes can be very cold, especially at night, even in the summer months. During the day, the sun can be strong, making it feel warm or even hot, but once the sun goes down, temperatures can drop quickly. This big difference between day and night temperatures means that people need to be prepared for all kinds of weather, often wearing layers of clothing to stay warm. Traditional

Andean clothing is made from alpaca or llama wool, which is very warm and perfect for the cold mountain weather. The wool is also water-resistant, helping to keep people dry when it rains or snows. Highlanders often wear ponchos, hats, and scarves made from this wool, adding color and warmth to their everyday lives.

Agriculture, or farming, is a key part of life in the Andes, but farming on steep mountain slopes is not easy. The Andean people have come up with innovative ways to grow crops in high altitudes where the land is rugged and rocky. One of the most famous techniques is called "terracing." Terraces are flat steps that are carved into the sides of mountains, creating levels where crops can be planted. By creating these terraces, farmers can make use of mountain slopes that would otherwise be too steep for farming. Terraces also help prevent soil from being washed away by rain and keep water from flowing too quickly down the mountainside. This ancient technique, which was used by the Inca and other civilizations, is still in use today. Common crops grown on terraces in the Andes include potatoes, corn, and quinoa. Potatoes, in particular, are a staple food in the Andes, and there are thousands of different kinds, each suited to a specific altitude and climate.

Water is a precious resource in the high Andes. Because of the cold temperatures, much of the water is stored in glaciers, which slowly melt to provide streams and rivers that flow down the mountains. These rivers are essential for farming, drinking, and other daily needs. The people of the Andes have developed clever systems to use water wisely. They build canals to bring water from the mountains to their fields and villages, and in some places, they use ancient irrigation systems that were designed centuries ago. In recent times, however, climate change has been causing glaciers in the Andes to shrink, which worries many Andean communities because they rely on these glaciers as a steady source of water. The highlanders are learning to adapt by finding new ways to manage water, but it remains a big challenge for the future.

Animals play a very important role in Andean highland life, and people in the Andes have long relied on animals such as llamas and alpacas. Llamas are used as pack animals to carry heavy loads over the steep and rocky trails of the Andes. They are strong, sure-footed, and can carry large amounts of goods, which makes them ideal for transporting supplies across the mountains. In addition to llamas, alpacas are raised for their wool, which is soft, warm, and highly valued. People use alpaca wool to make clothing, blankets, and other items to keep warm in the chilly mountain air. These animals are well adapted to the high altitudes, with thick fur to keep them warm and the ability to graze on tough grasses that grow in the Andean highlands. In addition to llamas and alpacas, some families also keep guinea pigs, or "cuy," which are a traditional source of food in the Andes.

One of the things that makes Andean culture special is the close connection that people have with nature and the mountains. Many people in the Andes believe that the mountains are sacred, filled with spirits or "apus" that watch over the land and the people. This belief goes back to ancient times, when the Inca and other Andean civilizations would make offerings to the apus to ask for protection, good weather, or successful harvests. Even today, people might leave small offerings, like coca leaves, food, or flowers, on mountain paths or at the base of a mountain as a sign of respect. Festivals and ceremonies are also held to honor the mountains and nature, showing gratitude for the resources that make life in the high altitudes possible.

The Andean highlands are rich in traditions, many of which have been passed down through generations. Music and dance are important parts of Andean culture, and traditional instruments like the charango, a small guitar-like instrument, and panpipes are often played at festivals and gatherings. Andean music often reflects the beauty and challenges of mountain life, with melodies that can be joyful or reflective. Traditional dances often tell stories about the mountains, the seasons, or the connection between people and the land. During festivals, people dress in colorful costumes, often decorated with bright patterns and designs that represent their community or heritage.

Living in high altitudes also means that Andean people have developed special ways of cooking and preserving food. Because of the cool temperatures, food can be stored for longer periods without spoiling. The Andean people have long used methods like drying and freeze-drying to preserve food. For example, they make a special type of freeze-dried potato called "chuño," which can be stored for months or even years. Chuño is made by leaving potatoes outside at night, where they freeze in the cold mountain air, and then letting them dry in the sun during the day. This process removes moisture from the potatoes, making them lightweight and easy to store or carry. Chuño can be rehydrated and cooked when needed, providing a reliable food source even in difficult times.

Education and community are also important parts of Andean highland life. In some remote mountain villages, schools are far away, and children may have to walk long distances to attend classes. However, education is valued, and many families work hard to make sure their children learn reading, writing, and other skills. Because life in the Andes requires teamwork and cooperation, children also learn valuable life skills from their families and communities, such as farming, weaving, and caring for animals. In many Andean communities, people share resources and help each other with tasks like building houses or harvesting crops, creating a strong sense of community. Neighbors often work together, and festivals and celebrations bring everyone together to share food, music, and stories.

In recent times, technology has begun to reach some Andean highland communities, bringing changes to daily life. Solar panels are being introduced in some villages, providing electricity for the first time. Roads have improved, making it easier to travel between mountain villages and nearby towns. The internet is slowly becoming available in more places, which allows people to stay connected and learn about the wider world. However, many highland communities are careful to hold onto their traditions, recognizing that these customs have helped them survive in the mountains for generations.

Health can be a challenge in the high Andes, where the cold, thin air and isolated locations can make it difficult to get medical care. Some villages have traditional healers, called "curanderos," who use plants and ancient practices to treat illnesses. Coca leaves, for example, are widely used in Andean culture to help with altitude sickness and provide energy. The leaves are not only chewed but also used to make teas and as offerings in ceremonies. Modern medicine has become more accessible in recent years, with clinics opening in some areas and doctors traveling to remote villages, but traditional remedies are still important and are often used alongside modern treatments.

Despite the challenges, people in the Andes have a deep sense of pride in their mountain way of life. The mountains are their home, and they see beauty and strength in the high-altitude landscapes that surround them. Many Andean highlanders feel a special connection to their land, the animals, and the mountains themselves. They are experts at finding balance with nature, knowing how to take what they need from the land without taking too much. This respect for the environment helps keep the mountains healthy and supports the plants, animals, and people who live there.

Living in the high altitudes of the Andes is not easy, but it has shaped a culture that is strong, resilient, and deeply connected to the natural world. The people of the Andes have found ways to adapt and thrive in one of the most challenging environments on the planet. From their food and farming techniques to their clothing and traditions, everything about life in the high Andes is a testament to human ingenuity and the power of community. The mountains may be tough, but for the people who call them home, the Andes are a place of beauty, history, and heritage.

Chapter 7: The Andes Weather and Seasons

The weather and seasons in the Andes Mountains are unlike those in many other places on Earth. Because the Andes stretch so far along South America—from Venezuela in the north all the way down to Chile and Argentina in the south—the weather varies greatly depending on where you are in the mountains. In some parts, it can feel like summer all year long, while in others, it may feel like winter even in the middle of the warmest months. The Andes are a mountain range that crosses different climates and zones, from tropical rainforests near the equator to freezing glaciers in the south. This variety makes the Andes one of the most unique and diverse regions when it comes to weather and seasons.

In the northern Andes, near countries like Venezuela, Colombia, and Ecuador, the climate is tropical, which means it stays warm throughout the year. Here, instead of having four seasons like summer, fall, winter, and spring, there are mainly two seasons: the wet season and the dry season. During the wet season, which usually lasts from November to April, heavy rains are common, and the rivers swell with water, bringing life to the lush forests. The rain can be intense, with thunderstorms and even the occasional landslide because of all the water flowing down the steep mountain slopes. The dry season, which runs from May to October, has much less rain, and the sun shines more often, making it easier to travel and enjoy the natural beauty of the mountains. Although it's still warm, the dry season feels different, with clear skies and a more relaxed atmosphere in the forests and valleys.

Moving further south into the central Andes, which run through countries like Peru and Bolivia, the climate begins to change. The central Andes are at a higher altitude, so temperatures tend to be cooler, especially at night. Here, just like in the northern Andes, people experience a wet season and a dry season. The wet season is from about November to March, when rain showers are frequent, especially in the afternoons. During this time, the mountains and valleys turn green as plants soak up the rain, and farmers plant crops like potatoes, corn, and quinoa. Rivers and lakes fill up, providing water for farming, drinking, and other daily needs. However, the wet season can also make life more challenging, as heavy rains may cause flooding, landslides, and muddy roads that make travel difficult.

The dry season in the central Andes, from April to October, is considered the best time for travel, hiking, and outdoor activities. The skies are mostly clear, and temperatures are mild during the day, though they can drop sharply at night. This time of year is especially popular for festivals and celebrations, as people enjoy the sunny, crisp weather. The famous Inca Trail, leading to Machu Picchu in Peru, is often hiked during the dry season because it's easier to walk on dry trails without the risk of slipping on mud or getting drenched by rain. In the dry season, the land looks different as well—the bright green of the rainy season fades a bit, but the views are still beautiful, with mountains rising against a backdrop of bright blue skies.

As we travel even further south, the Andes enter what's known as the southern region, which includes Chile and Argentina. Here, the seasons start to resemble those in places farther from the equator, with four distinct seasons: summer, fall, winter, and spring. This part of the Andes experiences a much colder winter than the northern or central regions, especially in the high-altitude areas and near the glaciers in Patagonia, the southernmost tip of the Andes. Winter here lasts from June to August, bringing snow, cold winds, and freezing temperatures, especially in the high mountains. Snowfall is common, and in some areas, the snow can be very deep, covering the landscape in white for months. Ski resorts in places like Chile and Argentina attract visitors who want to enjoy winter sports like skiing, snowboarding, and snowshoeing. Winter can be challenging for local communities, as the cold makes it harder to grow crops and people have to find ways to stay warm.

Summer in the southern Andes lasts from December to February, bringing warmer temperatures, especially in the valleys and lower elevations. During the summer, the snow melts, filling rivers and lakes with fresh water, and the landscape comes alive with greenery. This season is also a great time for hiking, exploring, and enjoying the incredible scenery of the Andes. However, even in summer, the weather in the high mountains can be unpredictable, and it's not unusual for temperatures to drop suddenly or for a snowstorm to appear out of nowhere. In Patagonia, the southernmost region of the Andes, the summer days are long, with sunlight lasting well into the evening. This gives people more time to explore and enjoy the landscapes, which include glaciers, turquoise lakes, and vast grasslands.

One of the most fascinating things about the Andes weather is the phenomenon of microclimates. A microclimate is a small area where the weather can be very different from the surrounding regions. In the Andes, microclimates are common because the mountains create all kinds of environments. For example, on one side of a mountain, it might be rainy and foggy, while on the other side, it could be dry and sunny. In the cloud forests of the eastern Andes, the weather is often misty and humid, with regular rainfall that supports a lush jungle environment. Just a few miles away, in the high deserts, it can be dry, with barely any rain throughout the year. Microclimates make the Andes a land of contrasts, where you can see snow-capped peaks, tropical rainforests, and dry deserts all within a short distance of each other.

Altitude plays a big role in the weather of the Andes. In general, the higher you go, the colder it gets, and the thinner the air becomes. This is why the tops of the Andes mountains are covered in snow, even in tropical regions near the equator. High-altitude areas, known as the "puna" zone, are mostly cold and windy year-round. In these areas, temperatures can drop below freezing at night, even in the summer, and plants and animals have to be very tough to survive. Only certain types of grasses, shrubs, and small animals like llamas and alpacas can live in these high-altitude zones. People who live in the puna have to bundle up to stay warm, and they often rely on warm clothing made from the wool of alpacas and llamas.

The Andes are also known for strong winds, especially in the southern parts near Patagonia. Here, winds can blow fiercely across the mountains and valleys, creating a harsh environment. In winter, these winds can make the already cold temperatures feel even colder, making it challenging to be outside for long periods. The winds also shape the landscape, creating unique rock formations and sweeping sand and snow across the mountains. In Patagonia, the winds are so strong that trees grow sideways, bent by the constant force of the wind over many years. These winds are part of what makes Patagonia such a wild and beautiful place, but they can also make travel difficult, as they often cause delays and can make hiking and climbing more dangerous.

In the lower valleys and plateaus of the Andes, the climate is milder, and these areas are where most people live. Towns and villages in these valleys experience more moderate temperatures, with warmer days and cooler nights. Here, farming is more common, and people can grow a variety of crops, thanks to the more predictable weather. The valleys are often shielded from the harshest weather by the surrounding mountains, creating a more comfortable environment for daily life. In these areas, people can grow crops year-round by adjusting to the rainy and dry seasons, and they are able to raise animals like chickens, pigs, and cows alongside traditional Andean animals like llamas and alpacas.

One interesting feature of Andean weather is the effect of El Niño and La Niña. El Niño and La Niña are climate patterns that occur in the Pacific Ocean and can change the weather in the Andes dramatically. During an El Niño event, which happens every few years, the waters of the Pacific Ocean warm up, affecting weather patterns around the world. In the Andes, El Niño can bring heavier rainfall, causing floods and landslides in some areas. Crops can be damaged, and communities may need to rebuild roads or homes after severe weather. La Niña, on the other hand, is the opposite pattern, where the Pacific waters cool down. This can lead to drier conditions in the Andes, sometimes causing droughts that make it hard for people and animals to find enough water. Both El Niño and La Niña are reminders of how connected the Andes are to the wider world, with weather patterns far away having a big impact on life in the mountains.

In recent years, climate change has been affecting the weather in the Andes. Glaciers in the Andes are shrinking due to warming temperatures, which is a serious concern for communities that rely on glacier meltwater for drinking, farming, and electricity. As glaciers melt, rivers and lakes are filled with extra water at first, but once the glaciers are gone, there may be less water available in the future. Climate change is also causing some parts of the Andes to experience more intense rainstorms, leading to more landslides and floods. Farmers are finding that traditional planting times are shifting, and they are experimenting with new ways to grow crops as the seasons and weather patterns change.

Throughout the Andes, the weather and seasons have shaped the way people live, work, and celebrate. Many Andean festivals are linked to the seasons and the cycles of rain and harvest. For example, Inti Raymi, the Festival of the Sun, is celebrated in Peru in June around the time of the winter solstice. This festival honors the sun god, Inti, and marks the start of a new agricultural cycle. In Bolivia, people celebrate Alasitas, a festival where they buy small replicas of things they hope to receive, like food, money, or good weather for crops. These festivals are times of joy and gratitude, reflecting the Andean people's deep connection to nature and the seasons.

Chapter 8: Volcanoes of the Andes

The Andes Mountains are home to one of the longest chains of volcanoes in the world, stretching across seven countries: Venezuela, Colombia, Ecuador, Peru, Bolivia, Chile, and Argentina. This volcanic region is part of the "Pacific Ring of Fire," a path along the Pacific Ocean where many of the world's active volcanoes are found. The Andes volcanoes are formed by tectonic plate activity—specifically, where the Nazca and South American plates meet and push against each other. When the oceanic Nazca Plate is forced beneath the continental South American Plate, it causes intense heat and pressure, leading to magma rising from deep within the Earth. Over millions of years, this has resulted in the formation of hundreds of volcanoes, which have played an important role in shaping the landscape, climate, and life in the Andes.

One of the most famous volcanoes in the Andes is Cotopaxi in Ecuador. Cotopaxi is one of the highest active volcanoes in the world, standing over 19,000 feet tall, with a nearly perfect cone shape that can be seen from miles away. Cotopaxi's snow-capped peak contrasts beautifully with the green valleys below, making it a spectacular sight. Cotopaxi has erupted many times throughout history, and its activity has impacted the surrounding regions. Because it is so tall, Cotopaxi's eruptions often send ash and gases high into the atmosphere, where winds can carry the ash for miles. This ash eventually falls to the ground and acts like a natural fertilizer, enriching the soil and helping plants grow. While Cotopaxi's eruptions have brought destruction at times, they have also contributed to the rich soil of the region, which supports farming and plant life.

Volcanoes in the Andes can vary greatly in their shape and size. Some, like Cotopaxi, are towering, cone-shaped stratovolcanoes with steep sides formed by layers of lava and ash. Others are shield volcanoes, which have a flatter, more dome-like shape and erupt with less explosive lava flows. Shield volcanoes, like those found in Chile, usually have slower, more predictable eruptions that don't produce huge clouds of ash or pyroclastic flows. The Andes also have many smaller cinder cone volcanoes, which are made up of small, rocky fragments piled up around a central vent. Cinder cones don't reach the massive heights of stratovolcanoes, but they still add to the diverse landscape of the Andes, each with its own unique features.

One of the most active volcanic areas in the Andes is the Central Volcanic Zone, which stretches from northern Chile through Bolivia and into southern Peru. This region is home to some of the tallest volcanoes in the world, such as Ojos del Salado, which rises to nearly 23,000 feet. Ojos del Salado, on the border between Chile and Argentina, is the tallest active volcano on Earth and is surrounded by a harsh, dry desert. This area gets very little rainfall, making it look almost like a lunar landscape. Despite its dry conditions, Ojos del Salado and other volcanoes in the Central Volcanic Zone continue to produce occasional eruptions, showing just how active this part of the Andes can be.

Volcanoes in the Andes have a major impact on the daily lives of the people who live nearby. Many Andean communities rely on the fertile soil that volcanic ash provides, as it contains important minerals that help crops like potatoes, corn, and quinoa grow. This volcanic soil is especially valuable in regions where farming is difficult, like the high-altitude plains of the Andes. However, living near an active volcano can be dangerous, as eruptions can happen with little warning. When a volcano erupts, it can release lava, ash, and toxic gases, as well as cause landslides and mudflows known as lahars. Lahars are one of the most dangerous volcanic hazards because they move quickly down mountainsides, sweeping up rocks, mud, and anything else in their path. For example, in 1985, the eruption of Nevado del Ruiz in Colombia caused a devastating lahar that buried the town of Armero, killing thousands of people. This tragic event is a reminder of the power of Andean volcanoes and the risks that come with living near them.

Many Andean cultures have a special relationship with volcanoes, viewing them as both powerful and sacred. Indigenous groups often see volcanoes as spirits or gods that must be respected and honored. For example, in the Quechua culture, volcanoes are sometimes thought of as apus, or mountain spirits, that watch over the people and the land. People may leave offerings to these volcano spirits, asking for protection from eruptions or giving thanks for the fertile soil and clean water that volcanoes provide. Even today, ceremonies and festivals are held in honor of volcanoes, especially in areas where volcanic activity is frequent. This respect for volcanoes is an important part of Andean culture, blending traditional beliefs with an understanding of the natural environment.

In recent years, scientists have been working to better understand and monitor the volcanoes of the Andes. Many Andean volcanoes are located near populated areas, so it's crucial to keep an eye on their activity to protect the people who live nearby. Volcanologists, who are scientists that study volcanoes, use a variety of tools to monitor these mountains. They set up seismometers to detect small earthquakes that often occur before an eruption, and they measure gas emissions, as certain gases can signal that magma is rising toward the surface. Satellite images are also used to observe changes in the shape of a volcano, which can indicate that pressure is building up inside. This information helps authorities make decisions about evacuating people or closing off certain areas during periods of increased volcanic activity.

The Andes is also home to some incredible volcanic features, such as hot springs, geysers, and fumaroles. Hot springs are pools of naturally heated water that are warmed by geothermal activity beneath the Earth's surface. People in the Andes often visit hot springs for relaxation, and they are believed to have healing properties. Geysers, like those found in El Tatio in northern Chile, are hot springs that erupt with jets of steam and hot water, creating an impressive sight. Fumaroles are openings in the Earth's crust that release steam and gases, often with a strong smell of sulfur. These features are reminders of the volcanic activity that lies beneath the Andes, and they attract visitors who want to see the power of nature up close.

Volcanoes in the Andes have also played a role in preserving history. Some volcanic eruptions have buried ancient settlements, leaving them hidden under layers of ash for centuries. For example, the eruption of the Quilotoa volcano in Ecuador about 800 years ago covered nearby areas in thick ash, preserving artifacts from ancient Andean cultures. In some cases, volcanic eruptions have frozen time, capturing snapshots of past life that archeologists can study to learn about the people who once lived in these areas. These preserved sites give us a glimpse into ancient civilizations and the ways in which they interacted with the powerful forces of nature around them.

The southern Andes, especially in Chile and Argentina, have many active volcanoes that are closely monitored. Chile has some of the most active volcanoes in South America, including Villarrica, Llaima, and Osorno. Villarrica, often called the "volcano with the glowing peak," has a lava lake at its summit, which can sometimes be seen glowing at night. Villarrica is a stratovolcano, meaning it has steep slopes and erupts both lava and ash. Its frequent eruptions make it a popular destination for adventurous travelers who come to see the molten lava and hike on the snowy slopes. However, due to its activity, Villarrica is carefully watched by scientists to make sure people stay safe. In recent years, Villarrica has had several eruptions, reminding everyone of its powerful presence.

In Patagonia, near the southern tip of the Andes, the landscape is marked by extinct and dormant volcanoes. While these volcanoes are no longer active, their shapes still define the landscape, with volcanic peaks rising over lakes, forests, and glaciers. These ancient volcanoes are a testament to the Andes' fiery history, showing that this region has been shaped by volcanic activity for millions of years. Some of these extinct volcanoes have collapsed to form craters, which have since filled with water to become beautiful crater lakes. These lakes, with their crystal-clear water and rugged surroundings, attract visitors from around the world who come to experience the wild beauty of Patagonia.

The Andes volcanoes also contribute to the region's rich biodiversity. The volcanic soil in the Andes is nutrient-rich, supporting a wide range of plant life that would struggle to grow in less fertile soils. Forests, grasslands, and unique ecosystems have developed in volcanic areas, providing habitats for many species of animals, birds, and insects. Some plants and animals have adapted to live near volcanoes, even using the warm volcanic soil or hot springs to survive in the colder mountain areas. For example, certain types of grasses thrive in volcanic soil, and animals like the Andean fox and the Andean condor can often be found in these volcanic regions, making the Andes a fascinating place for nature lovers.

Volcanoes in the Andes also produce valuable resources. The high temperatures inside active volcanoes create mineral-rich deposits, including metals like copper, silver, and gold. Over time, these minerals are brought closer to the surface by volcanic activity, where they can be mined. The Andes is one of the richest sources of minerals in the world, and mining is an important industry in countries like Chile and Peru. However, mining near active volcanoes requires special care to avoid the risks of eruptions and protect the environment. The challenge is to balance the need for resources with the protection of natural landscapes and the safety of communities living near these powerful mountains.

While volcanoes in the Andes can be dangerous, they are also a source of wonder and beauty. From towering, snow-capped peaks to lava lakes and steaming fumaroles, the Andes volcanoes offer endless opportunities for exploration and discovery. People living in the Andes have learned to adapt to their volcanic surroundings, respecting the mountains and understanding that their lives are deeply connected to the forces beneath the Earth. These volcanoes remind us of the power and unpredictability of nature, and they add to the mystery and majesty of the Andes Mountains, making this mountain range one of the most awe-inspiring places on the planet.

Chapter 9: Amazing Plants of the Andes

The Andes Mountains are home to an extraordinary variety of plants, many of which cannot be found anywhere else on Earth. This range of plants is due to the Andes' unique geography, which includes different climates and elevations from the tropical cloud forests to high-altitude plateaus and icy mountaintops. With such a mix of ecosystems, plants in the Andes have adapted to survive in challenging environments, from freezing temperatures to intense sunlight and steep, rocky soil. Some plants here have developed thick leaves to conserve water, others have short, tough stems to withstand strong winds, and some even grow close to the ground to avoid frost. The amazing diversity of plants in the Andes has made it one of the world's most important centers of plant biodiversity, contributing not only to the landscape's beauty but also to the culture and survival of the people who live there.

One of the most iconic plants of the Andes is the *puya raimondii*, also known as the "Queen of the Andes." This remarkable plant is known for its giant flower spike, which can grow up to 30 feet tall and may hold as many as 30,000 individual flowers. It can take up to 100 years for a *puya raimondii* to bloom, making it a rare sight, but when it does, it is an incredible spectacle. The plant's flowers attract pollinators like hummingbirds, which drink the nectar and help spread pollen from one plant to another. However, after it flowers, the *puya raimondii* dies, completing its long life cycle. This plant is adapted to survive in the harsh, high-altitude environment of the Andes, and it is considered an endangered species, found mainly in Bolivia and Peru. Protecting the *puya raimondii* is important not only because of its uniqueness but also because it supports other species in its ecosystem.

In the lower Andes, particularly in the cloud forests, you'll find an incredible variety of orchids. Orchids are beautiful, delicate flowers that come in all shapes, colors, and sizes, and the Andes are home to over 3,000 species. Some orchids grow on trees, with roots that dangle in the air, absorbing moisture from the humid atmosphere, while others grow on the ground. Cloud forests are ideal habitats for orchids because they provide plenty of moisture and shade. Orchids have evolved to attract specific types of pollinators, such as bees, butterflies, and hummingbirds, with each species often having a unique relationship with its pollinator. Some orchids even look like the insects that pollinate them, tricking them into visiting and spreading their pollen. The wide variety of orchids in the Andes not only adds to the beauty of these forests but also plays a role in supporting the region's biodiversity, providing food and shelter for insects and small animals.

Another fascinating plant is the *polylepis* tree, one of the highest-growing tree species in the world. *Polylepis* trees grow in high-altitude regions, often above 13,000 feet, where few other trees can survive. These trees have twisted, gnarled trunks covered in layers of papery bark that help protect them from the cold and drying winds. The bark also peels off in thin layers, giving the tree a unique, flaky appearance. *Polylepis* trees grow slowly, but they can form small forests called "islands" in the high Andean landscapes, creating unique habitats for animals and other plants. These trees provide shelter for birds like the Andean tit-spinetail and other species that are adapted to high-altitude environments. Local communities have long relied on *polylepis* wood for fuel, but overuse has led to the decline of these forests. Efforts to conserve and restore *polylepis* forests are now underway, as these trees play an important role in preventing soil erosion and supporting biodiversity in the Andean highlands.

In the drier parts of the Andes, especially in areas close to the Atacama Desert, cacti have found a way to thrive. One type of cactus commonly found here is the *cardón* cactus, which resembles the North American saguaro cactus with its tall, ribbed, column-like shape. These cacti can grow very tall, sometimes reaching over 20 feet, and are well-suited to the dry, rocky soil. The *cardón* cactus stores water in its thick, fleshy stem, allowing it to survive long periods without rain.

Its spines help protect it from being eaten by animals and also reduce water loss by shading the plant's surface. The *cardón* cactus produces bright flowers that attract pollinators, and its fruit is a food source for animals and local people. In fact, people in the Andes have used cacti for centuries as sources of food, medicine, and even building materials.

In the Andes' alpine regions, known as the *puna*, tough grasses and shrubs dominate the landscape. These plants, like the *ichu* grass, are specially adapted to the cold, windy conditions and the intense sunlight found at high elevations. *Ichu* grass has long, wiry blades that help it withstand the dry conditions and prevent frost damage. This grass is an important part of the Andean ecosystem, providing food for grazing animals like llamas, alpacas, and vicuñas. The people of the Andes also use *ichu* grass for roofing on traditional houses, as its tightly packed blades help insulate against the cold. *Ichu* and other high-altitude grasses have also become symbols of the resilience and strength of Andean life, showing how plants and people have adapted together to the harsh conditions of the *puna*.

One of the Andes' best-known plants is the coca plant, which has been cultivated by Andean people for thousands of years. Coca leaves have special compounds that help people cope with the high altitudes, as chewing the leaves can reduce fatigue, hunger, and the effects of altitude sickness. Coca leaves are also used in traditional medicine, and they play a significant role in Andean rituals and ceremonies. However, the coca plant is controversial because it is also used to produce illegal drugs. Still, in Andean culture, the coca leaf is respected for its natural properties and is considered a sacred plant. It's important to understand that the traditional use of coca leaves is very different from the processed forms used for illegal purposes. For Andean communities, coca leaves are a symbol of resilience and a reminder of their connection to the land and its resources.

In the Andean cloud forests, you can find an abundance of mosses, ferns, and bromeliads, which thrive in the humid, misty environment.

Bromeliads are plants related to pineapples, with rosettes of stiff leaves that often hold water, providing a mini-ecosystem for insects, frogs, and even small birds. Some bromeliads grow on the ground, while others are epiphytes, meaning they grow on trees without harming them. By catching and storing rainwater in their leaves, bromeliads create tiny pools that help support the diverse life of the cloud forest. This ability to hold water makes bromeliads important for conserving moisture in the ecosystem, especially during dry periods. Many types of bromeliads bloom with vibrant flowers, adding splashes of red, pink, or purple to the forest's green landscape, and attracting pollinators like hummingbirds, which help spread their pollen.

In addition to these fascinating plants, the Andes are home to a wide variety of medicinal plants used by local communities for generations. The people of the Andes have developed extensive knowledge about the healing properties of plants, using them to treat everything from fevers and colds to digestive issues and skin conditions. One such plant is *maca*, a root vegetable that grows in the high-altitude regions of Peru and Bolivia. *Maca* has been used for centuries as a source of energy and as a remedy for various ailments. Today, *maca* is known worldwide as a "superfood" because of its nutritional value and is often used in smoothies and health supplements. Another well-known medicinal plant is *yacon*, a root that is eaten for its sweet taste and used to manage blood sugar levels. These plants demonstrate the Andean people's deep understanding of their environment and how they have adapted to use the resources around them for health and survival.

The Andes are also known for their unusual "forests" of *giant ground rosettes*, plants that grow in a rosette shape close to the ground to conserve warmth and moisture. One example is the *espeletia*, which is found in the paramo, a high-altitude ecosystem in the northern Andes. *Espeletias* have thick, fuzzy leaves that protect them from the cold and trap moisture, allowing them to survive in the harsh, frosty environment. These plants can grow to several feet in height, with thick, stem-like bases that store water and nutrients. During the rainy season, *espeletias* produce bright yellow flowers that stand out against the misty landscape, providing food for pollinators. The *espeletia* is an important part of the paramo ecosystem, helping to regulate water flow and prevent erosion.

Throughout the Andes, plants play a crucial role in preventing soil erosion, which is a serious issue in mountainous regions with steep slopes. Trees, shrubs, and grasses all help stabilize the soil with their roots, which prevent landslides and protect water sources. Andean plants are also important for the climate, as they absorb carbon dioxide and release oxygen. Forests and other plant-rich areas in the Andes act as "carbon sinks," helping to slow down climate change by storing carbon that would otherwise be released into the atmosphere.

The plants of the Andes are not only beautiful but also essential to the people, animals, and ecosystems that depend on them. They provide food, shelter, medicine, and spiritual meaning to the Andean communities, who have learned to live in harmony with these unique plants. Each plant, from the towering *puya raimondii* to the tiny mosses of the cloud forest, contributes to the Andes' incredible biodiversity, making this mountain range one of the most ecologically rich and culturally important places in the world. As the Andes face challenges from climate change, deforestation, and overgrazing, conserving these amazing plants has become a top priority for scientists and local communities alike. The plants of the Andes remind us of nature's resilience and the intricate connections between people and their environment, inspiring efforts to protect and celebrate this remarkable part of the world.

Chapter 10: The People Who Live in the Andes

The people who live in the Andes are known for their deep connection to the mountains and the land. Living at high altitudes and in challenging environments, Andean communities have developed unique cultures, traditions, and ways of life that make them resilient and resourceful. Many of these communities are descended from ancient civilizations, like the Incas, who thrived in the Andes long before European explorers arrived. Today, the Andes are home to millions of people spread across several countries, including Colombia, Ecuador, Peru, Bolivia, Chile, and Argentina. Each of these regions has its own cultural differences, but they also share a strong bond to the land, with a lifestyle shaped by the mountains' high altitudes, steep slopes, and ever-changing weather.

One of the most famous Andean communities is the Quechua people, descendants of the ancient Incas. The Quechua are one of the largest Indigenous groups in the Andes, living mainly in Peru, Ecuador, and Bolivia. They speak Quechua, the same language spoken by the Incas, and they have preserved many ancient customs and beliefs. Quechua people live in small villages in the mountains, often in traditional homes made of adobe bricks, which are built from a mixture of mud and straw that dries hard in the sun. Adobe homes are great for the highlands because they keep the inside cool in the day and warm at night. Many Quechua communities also grow their own food, raising crops like potatoes, corn, and quinoa on steep, terraced fields. These terraces were originally built by the Incas, who designed them to make farming possible on the mountainous terrain. These terraces help prevent soil erosion and capture water, making it easier to grow food in areas that might otherwise be too dry or rocky.

Another important Andean group is the Aymara, who live mainly around Lake Titicaca in Peru and Bolivia. Like the Quechua, the Aymara have lived in the Andes for centuries, developing a culture closely tied to the land and the lake. Lake Titicaca is one of the highest navigable lakes in the world, and it holds a special place in Aymara mythology. According to legend, the first Inca, Manco Cápac, was born from the waters of Lake Titicaca. Many Aymara people still practice traditional farming and fishing, and they use boats made of reeds to travel across the lake. These reed boats, called *balsas*, have been used for thousands of years and are made by weaving together bundles of totora reeds, which grow along the lake's shores. The Aymara people also raise llamas and alpacas, which are important animals in Andean life, providing wool for clothing, as well as transportation for goods across the mountains.

The Andes are also home to communities of Afro-Andean people, particularly in Colombia and Ecuador. Descendants of enslaved Africans brought to the region during colonial times, Afro-Andean communities have developed their own unique cultures, blending African, Indigenous, and European influences. They are known for their vibrant music, dance, and festivals, which bring communities together in celebration. Many Afro-Andean people live in rural areas, working as farmers, fishermen, and artisans. They grow crops like sugarcane, bananas, and coffee, which thrive in the lower, warmer valleys of the Andes. Afro-Andean communities have made significant cultural contributions to Andean society, preserving music styles like marimba and bomba, which combine African rhythms with Andean and Spanish instruments.

Life in the Andes is shaped by the mountains, and Andean people have developed ways to adapt to the high-altitude environment. Because the air is thinner at higher altitudes, it has less oxygen, which can make breathing difficult. Over generations, Andean communities have adapted physically to life in high altitudes. Many people born in the Andes have larger lungs and a higher number of red blood cells, which help their bodies absorb oxygen more efficiently. Andean people also chew coca leaves, a practice that dates back to ancient times. Coca leaves contain natural compounds that help reduce fatigue and symptoms of altitude sickness. Coca leaves are an important part of Andean culture, used not only as a remedy for altitude but also in traditional rituals and ceremonies.

Andean culture is deeply spiritual, with a belief system that honors the natural world. The mountains, rivers, and lakes are considered sacred, and people believe they are protected by spirits called *apus*. These *apus* are thought to be mountain gods or spirits that watch over the people, providing protection and blessings. Andean people often make offerings to the *apus*, asking for good weather, healthy crops, and the well-being of their families. These offerings, called *despachos*, might include coca leaves, grains, flowers, and other small items, and they are carefully prepared to show respect and gratitude to the mountain spirits. Some communities also celebrate Inti Raymi, the Festival of the Sun, which dates back to Inca times and is one of the most important Andean festivals. Inti Raymi is held each June in Cusco, Peru, to honor Inti, the sun god, and to pray for a successful harvest.

The Andean people also have unique styles of clothing suited to the mountain climate. In colder areas, people wear ponchos and chullos (traditional hats with earflaps) made from llama and alpaca wool, which provides warmth and protection from the wind. The clothing is often brightly colored and decorated with intricate patterns, which have cultural significance. Each design can represent a different region, village, or family, and the patterns are passed down through generations. Women often wear layered skirts called *polleras*, which are both warm and comfortable for working in the fields. Traditional Andean textiles are not only practical but also a form of art, with each piece taking weeks or even months to weave. Weaving is a skill learned from a young age, and many Andean people take pride in creating their own clothing.

Food is another important part of Andean life. Many traditional Andean dishes are made from local ingredients, such as potatoes, corn, quinoa, and beans. Potatoes are especially significant in the Andes, where more than 4,000 different varieties can be found. The potato was first domesticated by ancient Andean cultures thousands of years ago, and it has remained a staple food ever since. Andean people have traditional ways of preserving food, such as freeze-drying potatoes to make *chuño*, which can last for months or even years without spoiling. *Chuño* is made by leaving potatoes out in the cold night air, then drying them in the sun. This process allows Andean communities to store food for the long, cold winter months when fresh crops may not be available. Another popular dish is *cuy*, or guinea pig, which has been raised as a source of protein in the Andes for centuries. Guinea pigs are often cooked on special occasions and are considered a delicacy in Andean culture.

Andean communities are known for their strong sense of community and cooperation. One important tradition is *ayni*, a system of mutual help and reciprocity. In *ayni*, neighbors help each other with tasks like planting, harvesting, and building, knowing that the help they give will be returned when they need it. This practice strengthens community bonds and ensures that everyone has support, especially during difficult times. *Ayni* is not just about work—it's a way of life that reflects Andean values of sharing and unity. Another important tradition is *minka*, which is similar to *ayni* but usually involves larger communal projects, like building a school or repairing roads. *Minka* brings the whole community together to work on a shared goal, benefiting everyone and reinforcing the importance of teamwork.

Many Andean people have preserved traditional crafts and skills, such as weaving, pottery, and silverwork. These crafts are often passed down through families and play an important role in the economy.

Tourists visiting the Andes are often drawn to colorful markets, where artisans sell handmade textiles, jewelry, and other items. Weaving, in particular, is a highly valued skill, with each region having its own distinctive patterns and techniques. The vibrant colors and designs of Andean textiles reflect the natural landscape, with dyes made from plants, minerals, and insects, such as the cochineal insect, which produces a bright red dye. Andean crafts not only provide a source of income but also help keep traditional knowledge and skills alive.

In recent years, more Andean people have moved to cities, like La Paz, Quito, and Lima, in search of jobs and educational opportunities. Life in the cities is very different from the rural villages, and many people try to balance modern lifestyles with their traditional culture. While some Andean customs and languages have been lost over time, there is a growing movement to preserve and celebrate Andean heritage. Schools and community centers are teaching younger generations about their history, language, and customs, so they can carry on the traditions of their ancestors. There are also festivals and events that bring people together to celebrate Andean music, dance, and food, helping to keep the culture vibrant in both urban and rural areas.

The Andes are also a place of incredible biodiversity, and many Andean communities are involved in protecting the environment. Some areas in the Andes are part of national parks and nature reserves, which protect rare plants, animals, and unique ecosystems. Local people often play a role in conservation efforts, using their knowledge of the land to help protect water sources, prevent deforestation, and preserve native species. Many communities practice sustainable farming methods, using traditional techniques that are less harmful to the environment. Some Andean farmers are part of cooperative groups that focus on organic and fair-trade farming, producing crops like coffee, cacao, and quinoa in a way that benefits both the environment and the farmers themselves.

Throughout their history, the people of the Andes have shown remarkable strength and adaptability, building societies that thrive in one of the most challenging environments in the world. Whether in the high mountain villages or bustling cities, Andean people continue to honor their ancient traditions while also embracing new opportunities. Their close relationship with the land, respect for nature, and sense of community make Andean culture truly unique. The people of the Andes remind us of the importance of resilience, cooperation, and living in harmony with the natural world. Their way of life is a testament to the power of tradition, adaptation, and respect for the environment, ensuring that the Andes remain not only a place of breathtaking landscapes but also a home for a vibrant and enduring culture.

Chapter 11: Hidden Treasures and Legends

The Andes are not just famous for their stunning landscapes and high mountains; they are also a place of mystery, filled with hidden treasures and legends that have captured people's imaginations for centuries. Stories of lost cities, sacred artifacts, and magical creatures are passed down from one generation to the next, blending history, mythology, and adventure. Many of these tales come from the ancient civilizations that once lived in the Andes, like the Incas, who left behind magnificent ruins, hidden paths, and stories of places that have yet to be discovered. Even today, explorers and archaeologists travel to the Andes, hoping to uncover secrets that may have been hidden for hundreds or even thousands of years.

One of the most famous Andean legends is the story of El Dorado, the "City of Gold." This legend began when Spanish explorers heard rumors about a king who would cover himself in gold dust and dive into a sacred lake as part of a ceremony. This tale of a golden king turned into a wild hunt for a city overflowing with gold and jewels. Explorers imagined El Dorado as a place where every building was covered in gold, and where enormous treasures were waiting to be discovered. Many expeditions set out to find this city of gold, with explorers searching through thick jungles, high mountains, and deep valleys. Some believed El Dorado was in Colombia, while others thought it might be hidden somewhere in the Andes of Ecuador, Peru, or Bolivia. Although no one ever found El Dorado, the legend continues, inspiring books, movies, and even more exploration. To this day, some people still wonder if there could be a hidden city filled with gold somewhere in the vast Andes.

Another fascinating treasure from Andean legend is the "Golden Chain of the Incas." According to stories, the Inca Empire once had a massive gold chain that was so heavy it took hundreds of men to carry it. This chain was supposedly created for a special ceremony when a new Inca king, or *Sapa Inca*, took the throne. The chain was said to be decorated with jewels and crafted from the purest gold, symbolizing the wealth and power of the Inca Empire. When the Spanish conquered the Incas, they heard rumors about this golden chain and wanted to find it for themselves. However, the chain was never found, leading people to believe that it was hidden by the Incas to keep it safe from the conquerors. Some say it was buried high in the mountains, while others believe it was thrown into a lake or hidden in one of the secret tunnels that connect different parts of the Andes. To this day, the Golden Chain of the Incas remains one of the Andes' greatest mysteries, a treasure that may still be out there, hidden in the mountains.

Lake Titicaca, one of the largest lakes in South America and the highest navigable lake in the world, is also a place surrounded by legends and treasures. According to Inca mythology, Lake Titicaca is where the first Inca, Manco Cápac, and his sister-wife, Mama Ocllo, emerged to start the Inca civilization. The lake is considered sacred, and many people believe it holds great treasures hidden beneath its waters. There are stories of temples and golden statues that were thrown into the lake to protect them from invaders. In recent years, divers have explored parts of Lake Titicaca and have found artifacts, like pieces of pottery and even stone structures, which suggest that there might be more to these stories than just myth. Some believe that there could be an entire lost city under the lake, waiting to be discovered.

The Andes are also filled with stories of hidden tunnels and secret passageways that were supposedly created by the Incas and other ancient civilizations. These tunnels, if they exist, are said to connect important sites like Cusco, Machu Picchu, and other sacred places. Legends claim that these tunnels were used to transport people and treasures safely, allowing them to move through the mountains without being seen. One of the most famous tunnels is said to stretch from Cusco, the ancient capital of the Inca Empire, all the way to Machu Picchu. People believe that these tunnels contain secret rooms filled with treasures, as well as mummies of Inca kings and priests. Some explorers and treasure hunters have tried to find these tunnels, but the mountains of the Andes are vast, and the supposed entrances are well hidden. Whether or not these tunnels exist, they add a sense of mystery to the Andes, making people wonder what other secrets might be waiting to be discovered.

Besides physical treasures, the Andes are also known for stories of magical creatures and powerful spirits. One of these legendary creatures is the *Ukumari*, a mysterious bear-like being that is said to live in remote areas of the Andes. According to legend, the *Ukumari* is not an ordinary bear; it is believed to have magical powers and is sometimes described as a protector of the forests and mountains. People who have encountered the *Ukumari* say it appears suddenly, then disappears into thin air. The *Ukumari* is respected and feared, and many Andean people believe it's a guardian of hidden treasures in the mountains. Another creature from Andean folklore is the *Amaru*, a giant serpent with wings that is said to live in caves or deep lakes. The *Amaru* is often depicted as both a dangerous and a wise being, capable of bringing good fortune to those who show it respect. These mythical creatures add to the sense of wonder and mystery in the Andes, reminding people that the mountains hold more than just physical treasures.

In addition to legends of treasure and creatures, the Andes are full of stories about magical plants and healing powers. The Incas and other Andean cultures believed that certain plants had special abilities, like the *ayahuasca*, a vine that was used in ceremonies to connect with the spirit world. Shamans, or healers, would drink a mixture made from the *ayahuasca* vine to gain visions and communicate with spirits. This sacred plant is still used in some Andean communities today, and it is respected as a powerful tool for healing and gaining wisdom. Another plant with legendary status is the coca leaf, which has been used by Andean people for centuries. Coca leaves are chewed to relieve altitude sickness, give energy, and connect people to the mountains. In Andean culture, coca leaves are also offered to the *apus*, the mountain spirits, as a sign of respect and gratitude. These plants are seen as gifts from the mountains, a part of the Andes' hidden treasures that help people connect with the natural world.

One of the most intriguing legends is that of Pachamama, the Earth Mother. In Andean beliefs, Pachamama is the goddess of fertility, harvest, and all things natural. Andean people believe that Pachamama watches over them, providing food, water, and everything they need to survive. In return, they show respect for the land by making offerings and celebrating festivals in her honor. Every August, many Andean communities hold a celebration to honor Pachamama, offering coca leaves, chicha (a traditional corn drink), and other gifts to thank her for the harvest. The mountains, rivers, and valleys are seen as her children, and people treat the land with great care to avoid offending her. For the Andean people, Pachamama is more than just a goddess; she is a constant presence, a reminder of the deep connection between humans and nature. This respect for Pachamama has helped shape Andean culture, making people more conscious of their relationship with the environment and the treasures it holds.

The Andes have also inspired legends about lost knowledge and wisdom. There are tales of ancient books or scrolls that supposedly contain secrets about the universe, nature, and human life. Some believe that these writings were hidden in caves or buried in remote parts of the mountains to protect them from invaders. These lost records are said to hold the wisdom of the ancient Andean people, including knowledge about medicine, agriculture, and spirituality. According to legend, only those who are pure of heart and respectful of the land can find these hidden treasures of knowledge. While no such records have been found, Andean culture is rich in oral traditions, with knowledge passed down through stories, songs, and rituals. This way, the wisdom of the past lives on, helping guide future generations in harmony with the mountains.

As people continue to explore the Andes, new discoveries are made every year, and yet much remains hidden or unexplained. Ancient ruins, mysterious rock formations, and unexplored caves hint at the countless stories and treasures the Andes still hold. Scientists and historians study these sites, but many Andean people believe that some secrets are meant to remain hidden, guarded by the mountains and the spirits of their ancestors. The Andes teach us that not all treasures are made of gold or jewels; some are found in the traditions, wisdom, and connections between people and nature. The Andes' legends and hidden treasures remind us of the mysteries that still exist in our world, waiting for those with courage, respect, and a sense of wonder to discover them.

Chapter 12: Famous Rivers and Lakes of the Andes

The Andes Mountains are home to some of the most famous rivers and lakes in South America, each one flowing with stories, mysteries, and natural beauty. These waterways are more than just places on a map; they are lifelines for the people, plants, and animals of the Andes. Many of them hold spiritual significance and have inspired myths, legends, and traditions passed down for centuries. The rivers and lakes of the Andes shape the landscape, carve deep valleys, create fertile lands for farming, and provide water to countless communities. They connect mountain villages, rainforests, and coastal deserts, linking different ecosystems and cultures across the continent.

One of the most well-known lakes in the Andes is Lake Titicaca, which lies between Peru and Bolivia. It's the largest lake in South America by volume of water and the highest navigable lake in the world, sitting at over 12,500 feet above sea level. For the people of the Andes, Lake Titicaca is much more than just a body of water—it is a place of deep spiritual importance. According to Inca mythology, Lake Titicaca is the birthplace of the first Inca king, Manco Cápac, and his sister-wife, Mama Ocllo, who were sent by the sun god, Inti, to start the Inca civilization. They are said to have emerged from the lake and went on to found the city of Cusco. This story makes Lake Titicaca a sacred site, and many Andean people still perform ceremonies by the lake's shores to honor their ancestors and the gods. The lake is also dotted with islands, some of which are believed to be home to ancient spirits. The most famous is the Island of the Sun, or Isla del Sol, where ruins of Inca temples can still be found. People from local communities, especially the Aymara and Quechua people, still visit these sites and pay respects to the lake's mystical energy.

Lake Titicaca is also known for its unique ecosystems. Its waters are home to a variety of wildlife, including species that aren't found anywhere else, like the Titicaca water frog. The people living around the lake have adapted to this environment, building reed boats and even floating islands made entirely from *totora* reeds, which grow along the lake's edge. The Uros people, an Indigenous community, live on these floating islands, maintaining a lifestyle that has been practiced for generations. They use the reeds to build their homes, boats, and even crafts that they sell to visitors. For the Uros and other communities, Lake Titicaca is a vital source of fish, water, and cultural identity, deeply connected to their way of life.

The Andes are also home to the mighty Amazon River, one of the longest and largest rivers in the world. Although the Amazon is mostly known for the rainforest, it actually begins high in the Andes. Its headwaters are located in Peru, where the river starts as small streams that gather and grow as they flow down the mountains. These small streams combine to form larger rivers, which eventually merge to become the Amazon. By the time the Amazon reaches Brazil, it is a powerful, massive river carrying a vast amount of water and nutrients into the rainforest. This incredible river provides life to the Amazon Rainforest, one of the most biodiverse places on Earth. From jaguars and pink river dolphins to countless fish, plants, and insects, the Amazon River sustains an astonishing variety of species. For the people living along its banks, the Amazon provides water, food, and transportation, making it an essential part of daily life in both the mountains and the rainforest below.

Another important river in the Andes is the Magdalena River, which flows through Colombia. The Magdalena is not as famous as the Amazon, but it is one of Colombia's most important rivers, both culturally and economically. It runs for over 950 miles, starting in the Andes and flowing north until it reaches the Caribbean Sea. The river passes through diverse landscapes, from the high Andes to tropical lowlands, and it supports a variety of wildlife, including manatees, fish, and bird species. For centuries, the Magdalena River has been a main route for transportation and trade, connecting remote Andean towns with larger cities along the coast. The people living along its banks have developed unique customs and traditions, celebrating festivals that honor the river's importance in their lives. Fishing, farming, and transportation all rely on the Magdalena's waters, and its fertile valley has allowed agriculture to thrive. The river is also a cultural icon in Colombia, inspiring music, literature, and art that reflects the deep bond between the river and its people.

One of the longest rivers that originates in the Andes and flows toward the Pacific Ocean is the Marañón River. Known as the "Grand Canyon of South America," the Marañón flows through a series of deep gorges and rugged canyons, carving its way through Peru's mountains. This river is one of the main sources of the Amazon and is crucial for bringing water down from the Andes into the rainforest. The Marañón is famous for its stunning scenery and wild rapids, making it a favorite destination for adventurers and kayakers. However, the river is also vital for local communities, who rely on its waters for irrigation, fishing, and even as a source of medicinal plants found along its banks. The river's importance has led to efforts to protect it from development, as it faces challenges from dam projects that could disrupt the natural flow and harm the surrounding ecosystems.

The Andes are also home to the Desaguadero River, which connects two important Andean lakes: Lake Titicaca and Lake Poopó in Bolivia. The Desaguadero flows south from Lake Titicaca, carrying water and nutrients into the high plains. Although the Desaguadero is not a very large river, it is vital for the local environment, as it helps maintain the balance of water in the highland ecosystem. Lake Poopó, however, has faced significant challenges due to climate change and water diversion, causing it to dry up several times in recent years. For the communities living near the lake, this has been a tragedy, as the lake was once an important source of fish and water. The story of Lake Poopó and the Desaguadero River serves as a reminder of the importance of protecting these fragile Andean water sources, which are essential for the survival of both people and wildlife.

Another notable river system is the Orinoco, which, like the Amazon, begins in the Andes. The Orinoco River flows mostly through Venezuela, but its origins are in the Andes of Colombia. It winds its way through vast plains and tropical forests, creating a rich environment that supports diverse wildlife, from giant river otters to caimans and piranhas. The Orinoco Basin is one of the most important ecological areas in northern South America, providing habitat for rare and endangered species. The river is also a crucial waterway for transportation, connecting remote communities and allowing them to trade goods with each other. The people who live along the Orinoco, including Indigenous groups, depend on the river for fishing, farming, and daily life, much like the people along the Amazon. The Orinoco River and its tributaries bring life to a wide area, shaping the land and culture of northern South America.

In the Andes, rivers and lakes are not only sources of water and food but also places of deep cultural and spiritual meaning. Many Indigenous communities believe that rivers and lakes have spirits, and they make offerings to these spirits to show respect and gratitude. For example, Andean people often perform ceremonies to honor the water, praying for healthy rivers, good weather, and plentiful harvests. These ceremonies might include offering coca leaves, flowers, and even small items to the water, asking for protection and blessings. The Andes' rivers and lakes are considered sacred, and people are taught from a young age to respect and protect them. This relationship with the water reflects a deep understanding of the importance of nature, as well as the belief that humans are connected to the environment in a powerful way.

The rivers and lakes of the Andes are not just natural wonders; they are the lifeblood of the mountains, sustaining the people, animals, and plants that call this region home. They flow through ancient lands, carry stories of the past, and inspire future generations to respect and protect the environment. Each river and lake has its own personality, from the icy headwaters in the high peaks to the lush valleys below, creating a complex network of waterways that bind the Andes together. As people continue to explore and learn about these famous rivers and lakes, they are reminded of the Andes' incredible diversity, history, and the need to preserve these precious resources for generations to come.

Chapter 13: How the Andes Were Formed

The Andes Mountains are one of the longest and highest mountain ranges in the world, stretching over 4,300 miles along the western edge of South America. Their formation is a fascinating story of powerful geological forces at work over millions of years, creating towering peaks, deep valleys, and rugged landscapes that continue to change today. The Andes were formed primarily by a process called tectonic plate movement, which involves giant slabs of Earth's crust moving and colliding. These tectonic plates—specifically the Nazca Plate and the South American Plate—played a key role in building the Andes, creating a range that is both awe-inspiring and scientifically significant. Understanding how the Andes formed gives us insight into how Earth's surface is shaped and transformed over vast periods of time.

The story of the Andes began over 200 million years ago, during a time when all of Earth's land was part of a supercontinent called Pangaea. Over millions of years, Pangaea began to split apart, creating separate continents. The South American continent drifted westward, eventually colliding with the Nazca Plate, a dense oceanic plate located in the Pacific Ocean. When these two plates collided, the lighter South American Plate rode up and over the heavier Nazca Plate. This collision forced the Nazca Plate to sink, or subduct, underneath the South American Plate in a process known as subduction. The intense pressure and friction caused by this subduction pushed up the Earth's crust, forming the Andes Mountains. This process of one plate sliding beneath another created a line of mountains and volcanoes that stretches along the continent's edge, forming the spine of South America.

The Andes are considered young mountains in geological terms, as they began to form about 50 million years ago. Compared to older mountain ranges like the Appalachians, which are hundreds of millions of years old, the Andes are still relatively new and continue to grow. The subduction of the Nazca Plate beneath the South American Plate still happens today, which means that the Andes are constantly being reshaped. Some parts of the Andes rise by several millimeters each year, creating a landscape that is always changing. Earthquakes, landslides, and volcanic eruptions are common in the region, as the tectonic plates continue to move and interact. These natural events are a reminder of the powerful forces that created the Andes and show how the mountains are still growing and shifting.

One of the most interesting features of the Andes' formation is the presence of volcanoes along the range. The subduction of the Nazca Plate beneath the South American Plate generates intense heat, which melts rock in the Earth's mantle and creates magma. This magma rises to the surface through cracks in the Earth's crust, forming volcanoes. The Andes are part of the "Ring of Fire," a zone of volcanic activity that encircles the Pacific Ocean. The Andean Volcanic Belt is divided into several sections, each with its own unique characteristics. Some of the tallest and most active volcanoes in the world are found in the Andes, like Cotopaxi in Ecuador, Ojos del Salado in Chile, and Misti in Peru. These volcanoes not only contribute to the mountain range's height but also play a role in shaping the Andean landscape by creating fertile soil, forming new land, and even influencing the climate.

The Andes Mountains are also shaped by erosion, a process that wears down the mountains over time. Wind, rain, ice, and rivers gradually erode the mountains, carving out valleys, cliffs, and canyons. During the last Ice Age, glaciers covered large parts of the Andes, slowly grinding down the rocks and creating U-shaped valleys and steep peaks. When the glaciers melted, they left behind lakes, rivers, and unique landscapes that are still visible today. Glaciers are still present in some parts of the Andes, especially in the southern regions, where they continue to shape the mountains by slowly moving and carving the land beneath them. The combination of tectonic uplift and erosion has created a rugged landscape, with sharp peaks and deep valleys that are a defining feature of the Andes.

In addition to tectonic forces and erosion, the Andes have been influenced by climate. The mountain range stretches through different climate zones, from the warm tropics near the equator to the cold and windy regions of Patagonia in the south. The tropical Andes are often covered in lush forests and receive heavy rainfall, while the higher altitudes are much colder and covered in snow. These varying climates contribute to the Andes' diverse ecosystems and affect how the mountains change over time. For example, in wetter areas, rivers and rain erode the mountains quickly, creating steep valleys and deep gorges. In colder areas, glaciers shape the mountains, while in drier regions, the mountains are more resistant to erosion, leading to unique rock formations and desert landscapes.

The Andes are made up of different types of rock, including volcanic rock, sedimentary rock, and metamorphic rock. Each type of rock tells a story about the Andes' formation and the environmental conditions that existed millions of years ago. Volcanic rock, for instance, is a result of volcanic eruptions that occurred during the mountains' formation. Sedimentary rock was formed from layers of sand, silt, and mud that were deposited in ancient seas and lakes before the Andes rose up. Over time, the pressure of tectonic forces transformed these layers into rock, which was then pushed up to form part of the mountains. Metamorphic rock was created when existing rock was subjected to extreme heat and pressure, changing its structure and appearance. The different types of rock in the Andes provide clues about the geological processes that shaped them and the environments that existed long before the mountains rose.

The Andes have also been affected by geological faults, which are cracks in the Earth's crust where sections of rock move. These faults, like the Liquiñe-Ofqui Fault in Chile, have caused powerful earthquakes throughout the Andes' history. Earthquakes happen when tectonic plates suddenly release built-up pressure, causing the ground to shake. The Andes experience frequent earthquakes, some of which are strong enough to reshape the land. These earthquakes create landslides, alter river paths, and even lift or lower sections of the mountains. In some cases, entire towns have been destroyed by Andean earthquakes, and new landscapes are created as the land shifts. Faults and earthquakes are a reminder of the Andes' active tectonic setting and how the mountains are constantly changing.

Another fascinating aspect of the Andes is how they have influenced the formation of other landscapes, such as the Amazon Rainforest. When the Andes rose, they acted as a barrier, blocking moist air from the Atlantic Ocean and causing heavy rainfall on the eastern slopes. This rainfall helped create the Amazon River and its vast rainforest, which is one of the most biodiverse places on Earth. Without the Andes, the Amazon Rainforest might not exist in its current form, showing how mountains can shape entire ecosystems beyond their borders. The Andes are essential to the climate and water cycle of South America, influencing rainfall patterns, river systems, and even the distribution of plants and animals across the continent.

The Andes continue to be studied by scientists, who are interested in learning more about how these mountains formed and how they continue to change. Researchers use technology like satellite imaging, seismic monitoring, and rock dating to study the Andes' geology and tectonic activity. By studying the Andes, scientists can learn more about the processes that shape Earth's surface and gain insights into how other mountain ranges formed. This knowledge is important not only for understanding Earth's past but also for predicting natural events like earthquakes and volcanic eruptions. The Andes offer a unique opportunity to study active tectonic processes in action, providing a natural laboratory for geologists and a chance to unravel the secrets of mountain formation.

For the people living in the Andes, these mountains are more than just geological formations—they are a part of their culture, history, and identity. Indigenous communities have long recognized the power of the Andes, often viewing the mountains as sacred and treating them with respect. In many Andean cultures, mountains are considered to have spirits, known as *apus*, which are believed to protect the people and provide them with resources. Andean communities live in harmony with the mountains, building terraced farms, constructing homes from local materials, and adapting to the challenges of high-altitude life. The Andes have shaped their way of life, influencing their agriculture, architecture, and spiritual beliefs. The mountains are a source of inspiration, beauty, and pride, representing the resilience and adaptability of the people who call the Andes home.

In summary, the Andes Mountains were formed by the collision and subduction of tectonic plates, specifically the Nazca Plate and the South American Plate. This process created a towering mountain range that continues to rise and change today. The Andes were further shaped by volcanic activity, erosion from glaciers and rivers, and the effects of climate and environmental conditions. Different types of rock within the Andes tell the story of ancient seas, volcanic eruptions, and intense pressure that transformed the landscape. Earthquakes and faults are still reshaping the Andes, reminding us of the immense geological forces at work. The mountains have influenced not only the South American landscape but also its ecosystems, culture, and climate. As scientists continue to study the Andes, they uncover more about Earth's past and gain valuable knowledge about the natural forces that create and shape mountain ranges across the globe. For Andean communities, the mountains hold a deep cultural significance, representing both the challenges and beauty of life in one of the world's most dramatic landscapes. The story of the Andes is a reminder of the powerful, ever-changing nature of our planet, as well as the incredible resilience of the people and wildlife that call these mountains home.

Chapter 14: Animals That Live at the Top

The Andes Mountains are filled with fascinating animals, and some of the most unique creatures live at the very top of this towering range, where the air is thin, the temperatures are low, and the winds can be fierce. Life at these high altitudes isn't easy, and animals that call the top of the Andes home must be specially adapted to survive in such a challenging environment. With limited food, freezing nights, and less oxygen than at lower levels, these animals have developed incredible features and behaviors to help them thrive. From mammals with thick fur coats to birds with extraordinary wings, the Andes are home to creatures that have learned to live in one of the harshest environments on Earth. These high-altitude animals not only survive but also play essential roles in their ecosystems, contributing to the unique balance of life in the Andes.

One of the most iconic animals that live at the top of the Andes is the Andean condor, one of the largest flying birds in the world. With a wingspan of up to 10 feet, the Andean condor soars high above the mountains, using thermal air currents to glide without expending too much energy. This bird is a type of vulture, meaning it primarily feeds on carrion, or the remains of dead animals. By consuming carrion, the condor helps keep the environment clean and prevents the spread of disease. The Andean condor is well-suited to the high-altitude life of the Andes. It has powerful wings that allow it to glide for hours without flapping, conserving its energy in the thin mountain air. Condors are also highly social birds, often gathering in groups to roost on high cliffs, which offer them a safe place to rest and an excellent vantage point for spotting food. Their role as scavengers makes them important to the ecosystem, as they help recycle nutrients back into the environment. The Andean condor is a symbol of power and freedom in many South American cultures, and although they are endangered due to habitat loss and human threats, efforts are underway to protect these magnificent birds.

Another remarkable animal that lives at the top of the Andes is the vicuña, a wild relative of the llama and alpaca. Vicuñas are known for their extremely soft and fine wool, which helps them stay warm in the chilly mountain temperatures. Unlike their domesticated cousins, vicuñas are wild animals and can be very shy. They are well adapted to the high altitudes, with a specialized heart and lungs that allow them to survive on the low oxygen levels found in the mountains. Vicuñas graze on tough grasses and plants that grow in the high Andes, and they have a unique way of living in family groups led by a dominant male. These groups are very protective of each other, and if a predator, like a puma, approaches, they make loud warning calls to alert the group. Vicuñas have also been important to Indigenous people of the Andes for centuries, as their wool, which is one of the finest and most expensive in the world, is harvested carefully without harming the animals. This wool was once reserved for Inca royalty, showing the high value placed on these beautiful animals.

Llamas and alpacas, though often found at lower elevations, are also adapted to life in the Andes and can be seen at high altitudes. Both animals are domesticated versions of wild species that have been used by Andean people for thousands of years. Llamas are strong and sturdy, making them perfect for carrying heavy loads across the mountains, while alpacas are raised primarily for their wool. These animals have thick, warm coats that protect them from the cold, and their feet are padded to help them walk on rocky terrain without slipping. Llamas and alpacas also have a unique way of conserving water in the dry mountain climate; they can go for long periods without drinking by getting moisture from the plants they eat. The connection between llamas, alpacas, and the Andean people is deep, as these animals provide transportation, clothing, and companionship to the communities living in the mountains.

The Andean mountain cat is one of the rarest and least-known animals in the Andes, making its home in some of the highest and most remote areas. This small, wild cat has a thick, soft coat with a beautifully striped tail, which helps it stay warm in the cold mountain air. The Andean mountain cat primarily hunts small mammals, such as chinchillas and viscachas, which are rodents that also live in the high-altitude grasslands. This elusive cat is a master of camouflage, blending into the rocky landscape to avoid detection by both predators and prey. Very little is known about the Andean mountain cat due to its secretive nature and the challenging conditions of its habitat, but conservationists are working to protect it. This species is considered endangered due to habitat loss and human threats, and efforts are being made to preserve its environment to ensure its survival.

Another high-altitude specialist is the spectacled bear, the only bear species native to South America. Although it can live in various habitats, the spectacled bear is often found in the cloud forests and high-altitude grasslands of the Andes. It gets its name from the white markings around its eyes, which resemble spectacles or glasses. The spectacled bear is an omnivore, which means it eats both plants and animals. Its diet mainly consists of fruits, plants, and small animals, but it can also climb trees to gather food, such as berries and leaves. The spectacled bear plays an important role in its ecosystem by helping to disperse seeds throughout the forest as it travels and feeds. These bears are very shy and elusive, often avoiding humans, but they are highly respected in Andean culture. In fact, the spectacled bear is the inspiration behind many myths and legends, often seen as a protector of the forest.

The Andean fox, also known as the culpeo, is another remarkable animal that thrives at high altitudes. This fox is well adapted to the tough conditions of the Andes, with thick fur to keep it warm and sharp senses that help it hunt for food in the rocky landscape. The Andean fox has a diverse diet, feeding on small mammals, birds, insects, and even fruits. Its adaptable nature allows it to survive in various habitats, from dry, desert-like areas to high-altitude grasslands. The Andean fox plays a key role as a predator in its environment, helping to control populations of smaller animals and maintain a healthy balance in the ecosystem. The fox is also part of Andean folklore, where it is often seen as a clever and resourceful animal. Because of its adaptability and resilience, the Andean fox has managed to survive despite the challenges posed by its habitat and human encroachment.

In the icy peaks and high-altitude wetlands, you can also find the Andean flamingo, one of the rarest flamingo species in the world. Unlike most flamingos, which are associated with warm, tropical environments, the Andean flamingo lives in cold, high-altitude lakes where the water is often salty or alkaline. These lakes are typically found in isolated areas, which helps protect the flamingos from predators but also means they have limited options when it comes to feeding. Andean flamingos feed on algae and small crustaceans that live in the salty water, using their specialized beaks to filter food. They are known for their stunning pink plumage, which comes from pigments in the algae and crustaceans they eat. Andean flamingos are considered vulnerable due to habitat loss and climate change, which affect the lakes they rely on for food and nesting.

Another high-altitude bird of the Andes is the giant hummingbird, the largest species of hummingbird in the world. Found at elevations of up to 15,000 feet, the giant hummingbird is adapted to the cold temperatures and thin air of the high Andes. Unlike its smaller relatives, the giant hummingbird has a slower wing beat and a longer lifespan. It feeds on nectar from Andean flowers, helping to pollinate the plants and contributing to the health of the ecosystem. Because of its large size and slower flight, the giant hummingbird is not as agile as other hummingbirds, but it has a unique grace as it hovers near flowers. This bird is a true marvel of adaptation, showcasing the resilience of life in the harshest conditions.

The Andean goose is another species well-suited to high-altitude life, often found near cold, glacial lakes. With a thick layer of feathers to insulate it from the cold and a strong, sturdy build, the Andean goose is perfectly adapted to the chilly, windy conditions of the high Andes. It feeds primarily on grasses and plants that grow in the mountain grasslands, and it often forms large flocks, which provide protection and warmth during the cold nights. The Andean goose is also an important part of local traditions and is sometimes seen as a symbol of good fortune for Andean farmers. Despite the challenges of living in such an extreme environment, these geese thrive, demonstrating how animals adapt to even the toughest landscapes.

Finally, we have the viscacha, a small rodent that resembles a rabbit and is a close relative of the chinchilla. Viscachas are social animals, living in colonies in rocky outcrops where they can find shelter from the cold and predators. They have thick, soft fur to keep them warm, and they are excellent climbers, moving easily among the rocks. Viscachas feed on grasses, leaves, and moss, which are some of the few plants that grow at high altitudes. These rodents are a crucial food source for predators like the Andean mountain cat and foxes, making them an important link in the Andean food chain.

Life at the top of the Andes is challenging, but the animals that live there have developed unique adaptations that allow them to survive and thrive in this extreme environment. From the soaring Andean condor to the elusive Andean mountain cat, each animal plays a role in the ecosystem, helping to maintain the delicate balance of life. These creatures have adapted to the thin air, cold temperatures, and limited resources in remarkable ways, showing how diverse and resilient nature can be. The animals of the high Andes are a testament to the power of evolution and the beauty of life in even the harshest conditions, making the Andes a truly extraordinary place for wildlife.

Chapter 15: Andean Traditions and Cultures

The Andean region is not only home to dramatic landscapes and unique wildlife but also rich with ancient traditions and cultures that have been shaped by the mountains, valleys, and high-altitude life. The people of the Andes have created a culture that celebrates their close connection to nature, their ancestors, and their communities. Many of these traditions date back thousands of years, influenced by powerful civilizations like the Inca Empire, and even before that by smaller Indigenous groups who found ways to thrive in this challenging environment. Today, Andean culture is a vibrant mix of old and new, blending Indigenous beliefs and customs with Spanish influences from colonial times. Celebrations, rituals, music, art, and festivals are all an essential part of life in the Andes, helping communities maintain their identity and pass down their heritage to future generations.

One of the most important aspects of Andean culture is the belief in *Pachamama*, or Mother Earth. Pachamama is considered the goddess of the earth, fertility, and the harvest, and she is believed to provide everything needed for life—food, water, shelter, and the beauty of nature. People in the Andes have a deep respect for Pachamama and honor her with rituals to show gratitude and seek her blessings. One of the most well-known rituals is the *pago a la tierra*, or payment to the earth. This offering ceremony is performed to thank Pachamama and ask for good crops, good health, and protection. People create offerings that include items like food, flowers, coca leaves, and sometimes even small animals, placing them in the ground or on special altars. These offerings are given with love and respect, reflecting the Andean people's strong bond with the land.

The Andean belief system also includes the worship of *apus*, or mountain spirits. Mountains are seen as sacred beings with their own spirits, often considered protectors of the land and the people who live there. Each community has its own *apus*, specific mountains that are believed to watch over them and provide guidance. People make offerings to the *apus* to seek protection, good fortune, and strength. This deep connection with the mountains comes from centuries of living in such close proximity to them, and the Andean people view these towering peaks with awe and reverence. The worship of *apus* is still practiced today, especially by Indigenous communities, showing how these ancient beliefs have remained a vital part of Andean identity.

The Andes are famous for their vibrant festivals, many of which are celebrated with music, dance, colorful clothing, and traditional foods. These festivals often blend Indigenous customs with Christian influences, a legacy of Spanish colonization. One of the most famous Andean festivals is Inti Raymi, or the Festival of the Sun. This celebration dates back to the Inca Empire and was held in honor of Inti, the sun god, who was believed to be the father of the Inca people. Inti Raymi is celebrated on the winter solstice, the shortest day of the year, as a way to honor the sun and ensure its return to provide warmth and light. Today, Inti Raymi is celebrated in Cusco, Peru, with elaborate ceremonies, reenactments, traditional music, and dancing. Thousands of people gather to watch the celebrations, which are led by actors playing the roles of Inca rulers and priests. Inti Raymi is a powerful reminder of the Inca Empire's legacy and the importance of the sun in Andean culture.

Carnival is another major festival celebrated throughout the Andes, and it is a lively and colorful event that takes place before Lent, a period of fasting and reflection in Christianity. Andean Carnival combines Indigenous and Spanish traditions, with parades, music, dancing, and vibrant costumes. People often wear masks and dress in bright colors, filling the streets with energy and joy. One of the most famous Carnival celebrations in the Andes is in Oruro, Bolivia, where thousands of dancers and musicians perform traditional dances, including the *Diablada*, or Dance of the Devils. This dance tells the story of the struggle between good and evil, and the performers wear elaborate costumes and masks representing devils, angels, and other mythical creatures. Carnival is a time for communities to come together, celebrate life, and honor their heritage through music and dance.

Music is an essential part of Andean culture, with instruments like the *charango* (a small guitar-like instrument), *quena* (a traditional flute), and panpipes creating the unique sounds of Andean music. These instruments have been used for centuries, with origins that trace back to pre-Inca times. Andean music often has a haunting, melodic quality that reflects the beauty and mystery of the mountains. Traditional songs are played at festivals, ceremonies, and community gatherings, helping to keep Andean culture alive. The music often tells stories of the land, the people, and their connection to nature, carrying deep meanings that go beyond the notes themselves. Musicians are highly respected in Andean communities, as they play a key role in passing down cultural knowledge and history through their songs.

Traditional clothing is another important part of Andean culture, with vibrant colors and intricate designs that reflect the heritage of each community. Many Indigenous Andean people wear clothing made from alpaca and llama wool, which is warm and ideal for the cold mountain climate. Women often wear brightly colored skirts called *polleras*, layered over each other, along with shawls, hats, and woven belts. The designs on these garments are not just decorative—they often represent symbols, animals, or natural elements important to the Andean people. Each region has its own style of clothing, and these traditional garments are worn with pride, especially during festivals and ceremonies. Weaving is a skill passed down through generations, and Andean weavers are known for their exceptional craftsmanship and the detailed patterns they create. The art of weaving is more than just a craft; it is a way for Andean people to express their identity, values, and relationship with the natural world.

One of the oldest traditions in the Andes is agriculture, which has been practiced for thousands of years. Farming at such high altitudes is challenging, but the Andean people developed techniques that allowed them to grow crops like potatoes, quinoa, and maize in the steep, rocky terrain. One of their most ingenious innovations is terracing, where fields are built in steps along the mountainsides. These terraces help prevent soil erosion, conserve water, and create flat areas for planting. Andean farmers also use a traditional crop rotation system that helps keep the soil healthy and productive. Potatoes, in particular, have a special place in Andean culture, as the Andes are the birthplace of this versatile vegetable. There are over 4,000 varieties of potatoes in the Andes, each with unique flavors, colors, and uses. Farming is not just a means of survival—it is deeply tied to Andean traditions and reflects the people's close connection to the land.

The Andes are also known for their unique culinary traditions, which combine Indigenous ingredients with Spanish influences. Traditional Andean dishes often include potatoes, corn, quinoa, and other crops that grow well in high-altitude climates. One popular dish is *chuño*, a freeze-dried potato product made by leaving potatoes out in the cold Andean nights and then drying them in the sun. Chuño can be stored for long periods and is an important food source during times when fresh crops are scarce. Another traditional food is *cuy*, or guinea pig, which has been a source of protein in the Andes for centuries. While it may seem unusual to some, cuy is a delicacy in many Andean communities and is often prepared for special occasions. Andean cuisine is a blend of flavors and techniques that reflect the region's history, environment, and cultural diversity.

The Andean people also have a strong tradition of storytelling and oral history. Stories, myths, and legends are passed down from generation to generation, preserving the history and wisdom of the past. Many Andean stories feature animals, spirits, and supernatural beings, and they often contain lessons about respect for nature and the importance of community. One popular Andean myth is the story of *Viracocha*, the creator god, who is said to have formed the world and all living things. According to the legend, Viracocha traveled across the Andes, teaching people and bringing order to the world. These stories are more than just entertainment; they are a way for Andean communities to keep their culture alive and share important values with younger generations. Storytelling is often accompanied by music and dance, creating a rich cultural experience that connects people to their roots.

In addition to these traditions, Andean people have a deep sense of community and reciprocity. One of the core values in Andean culture is *ayni*, a principle of mutual aid and cooperation. Ayni means that people help each other without expecting immediate rewards; instead, they know that support will be returned in the future. This sense of reciprocity is essential in the Andes, where farming and survival require teamwork. During the planting and harvesting seasons, entire communities come together to work in each other's fields, sharing the workload and celebrating with feasts and music. Ayni extends beyond agriculture, influencing social relationships, family ties, and even the construction of homes and public buildings. This cooperative spirit strengthens Andean communities and fosters a sense of unity and shared responsibility.

Throughout the Andes, ancient customs coexist with modern influences, creating a culture that is both timeless and adaptable. Many Andean people still practice traditional lifestyles, but they also incorporate modern technology, education, and global trends into their lives. This blending of old and new can be seen in everything from traditional clothing worn alongside modern fashion to festivals that include both Indigenous and Christian elements. Andean culture is a powerful reminder of resilience, adaptability, and the enduring strength of tradition. Even as the world changes, Andean communities continue to honor their roots, celebrating the beauty and wisdom of their ancestors while looking forward to the future.

In summary, Andean traditions and cultures are a beautiful mosaic of beliefs, practices, and values that have been passed down through generations. From honoring Pachamama and the mountain spirits to celebrating festivals with music and dance, the Andean people have created a culture that celebrates life, nature, and community. Their respect for the land, their intricate art and music, and their commitment to helping one another reflect a deep sense of connection to both their ancestors and the natural world around them. This culture has endured for thousands of years and continues to thrive in the modern world, preserving a legacy of resilience, harmony, and pride in the high mountains of the Andes.

Chapter 16: Challenges of Climbing the Andes

Climbing the Andes Mountains is a thrilling and challenging adventure that draws explorers, hikers, and mountaineers from all around the world. But the Andes aren't just any mountains—they are the longest continental mountain range on Earth, stretching over 4,300 miles through seven countries in South America. The terrain is rugged and diverse, from towering snowy peaks to dry deserts, deep valleys, and dense forests. These mountains test climbers with their unpredictable weather, high altitudes, and often remote locations. Climbing the Andes isn't easy; it requires physical and mental preparation, careful planning, and respect for the natural forces that shape these incredible mountains. For many, however, the challenge of reaching these high peaks, experiencing the breathtaking views, and connecting with the mountain landscape makes every difficulty worth it.

One of the biggest challenges in the Andes is the high altitude. Many of the Andes' peaks reach over 20,000 feet, with Mount Aconcagua in Argentina towering at nearly 23,000 feet. At such high altitudes, the air is much thinner, meaning there is less oxygen available for climbers to breathe. This can lead to altitude sickness, which happens when the body struggles to adapt to the lower oxygen levels. Altitude sickness can cause symptoms like headaches, nausea, dizziness, fatigue, and shortness of breath. In severe cases, it can lead to dangerous conditions like high-altitude pulmonary edema (HAPE) or high-altitude cerebral edema (HACE), where fluid builds up in the lungs or brain. To avoid these risks, climbers have to take time to acclimate, which means they stop at various points along the way to let their bodies get used to the altitude. This process can take several days, slowing down the climb, but it's essential for staying safe in the high Andes.

Another major challenge is the weather. The Andes experience a wide range of weather conditions, and the climate can vary dramatically depending on the region and time of year. Some parts of the Andes, like the dry Atacama Desert, are known for their lack of rainfall, while other areas receive heavy rain and snow. The higher altitudes are often cold, with temperatures dropping well below freezing, especially at night. On some peaks, temperatures can fall to -30°F (-34°C) or lower, which can cause frostbite and hypothermia if climbers aren't properly equipped. The Andes also face powerful winds that can suddenly pick up, making it difficult to maintain balance and navigate safely. These winds can be especially fierce at higher altitudes, where there is little vegetation to block them. In addition, sudden storms are common in the Andes, bringing rain, snow, and even lightning. Climbers have to be prepared for these extreme conditions, carrying gear that includes warm clothing, sleeping bags, and sturdy tents to withstand the mountain's intense weather.

The Andes' challenging terrain is another factor that makes climbing difficult. The landscape is diverse and often unpredictable, with rocky slopes, glaciers, steep cliffs, and narrow paths. Some mountains have loose rocks and gravel that can make footing unstable, increasing the risk of slipping or falling. On higher peaks, glaciers and snowfields are common, and climbers may need to use crampons (spiked metal plates worn on boots) and ice axes to safely move across icy surfaces. Glaciers can also have deep crevasses, which are large cracks in the ice that are sometimes hidden by snow, making them dangerous to cross. Skilled climbers often use ropes and harnesses to navigate these tricky areas, and they may travel in teams to support each other in case someone needs help. Navigating the steep slopes and icy patches requires experience, strength, and a good understanding of mountain safety.

Another challenge that climbers face in the Andes is the isolation and remoteness of many mountain areas. Unlike more popular mountain ranges where there are established routes and support systems, the Andes has vast stretches of wilderness with limited infrastructure. This means that climbers often have to carry all their supplies, including food, water, and camping gear, because they can't rely on finding resources along the way. Many Andean mountains are located far from towns or villages, so if something goes wrong, help might be hours or even days away. This isolation adds to the sense of adventure but also means climbers have to be extra cautious and prepared. Communication can be challenging in remote parts of the Andes, and climbers might need to carry satellite phones or emergency beacons to stay in contact with rescue teams. Knowing how to survive and take care of themselves in the wilderness is an important skill for anyone attempting to climb the Andes.

Climbing the Andes also requires a lot of physical strength and endurance. The journey to the top can take days or even weeks, depending on the route and the mountain. Climbers have to be prepared to walk long distances, sometimes uphill for hours, carrying heavy backpacks with all their gear. The thin air at high altitudes can make even small tasks feel exhausting, and climbers need to keep pushing forward despite the fatigue. Many climbers train for months before attempting to climb the Andes, building up their stamina, strength, and mental toughness. They often practice hiking, carrying heavy loads, and even training at high altitudes to prepare their bodies for the challenge. Good physical conditioning is essential, but mental strength is just as important. Climbers need to stay focused, stay positive, and keep going even when they're tired or facing tough conditions.

One of the less visible but very real challenges in the Andes is the need to protect the environment. As more people are drawn to climb these famous mountains, there is a risk of damaging the natural landscape. Climbers are encouraged to follow the principles of "leave no trace," meaning they take all their trash with them, avoid damaging plants, and respect the wildlife. Some areas in the Andes are home to rare plants and animals, and disturbing their habitats can have a lasting impact. Many climbers are committed to protecting the environment and work hard to make sure that the beauty of the Andes is preserved for future generations. Responsible climbers avoid littering, stay on designated trails, and make sure to clean up after themselves, showing respect for the land and the local communities who live nearby.

In addition to these natural challenges, climbers in the Andes may face difficulties due to cultural and language differences. The Andes span several countries, and climbers may need to navigate different languages, customs, and ways of life. Many people in the Andes speak Spanish, but in remote areas, especially in places where Indigenous communities live, people may speak Quechua or Aymara, languages with deep cultural roots. Being respectful and open to local traditions can help climbers form positive relationships with the communities they encounter. In some areas, local people serve as guides, sharing their knowledge of the mountains and providing support along the way. Building these connections can make the experience more meaningful and enrich climbers' understanding of Andean culture.

For climbers who make it to the top, the reward is incredible. From the high summits, they can see breathtaking landscapes that stretch for miles, with views of other peaks, valleys, glaciers, and sometimes even the vast Amazon rainforest in the distance. The sense of accomplishment after facing the Andes' challenges is unmatched, and many climbers describe the experience as life-changing. Reaching the top of an Andean peak is not just about physical achievement; it's also about connecting with nature, experiencing the beauty and power of the mountains, and pushing personal limits. The journey can be difficult, but for those who succeed, it's an unforgettable adventure that they carry with them forever.

In the end, climbing the Andes is not just about reaching the summit—it's about the journey, the teamwork, and the respect for nature and culture. Climbers come to the Andes not only to challenge themselves but also to learn from the mountains and the people who have called them home for thousands of years. The Andes demand respect, patience, and courage, and they offer rewards that go beyond words. For many, these mountains become a place of inspiration, a source of wonder, and a reminder of the strength of the human spirit.

Chapter 17: Famous Cities in the Andes

The Andes Mountains are not only famous for their stunning natural beauty and towering peaks but are also home to some remarkable cities filled with history, culture, and unique attractions. These cities offer a glimpse into the past and a vibrant mix of old traditions with modern life, set against the breathtaking backdrop of the Andes. Each of these cities has a unique story to tell, shaped by the geography of the mountains, the influence of ancient civilizations, and the blend of Indigenous and colonial cultures. From colorful festivals to ancient ruins and bustling markets, the cities in the Andes are full of life and adventure. Let's explore some of the most famous cities in the Andes and discover what makes each one so special.

Cusco, Peru, is perhaps one of the most well-known cities in the Andes. Often called the "Heart of the Inca Empire," Cusco was once the capital of the powerful Inca civilization. This ancient city is located high in the Andes, around 11,200 feet above sea level, and it's known for its well-preserved architecture, blending Inca stonework with Spanish colonial buildings. Walking through the streets of Cusco is like stepping back in time, as you can still see the original Inca walls in some parts of the city. These walls are made from massive stones that fit together so perfectly that not even a blade of grass can fit between them. Today, Cusco is a UNESCO World Heritage site and a popular starting point for tourists visiting Machu Picchu, the famous Inca citadel. In Cusco, visitors can explore the impressive Sacsayhuamán fortress, which overlooks the city, and enjoy the vibrant festivals that celebrate both Inca and Catholic traditions. Inti Raymi, the Festival of the Sun, is one of the biggest celebrations in Cusco, honoring the ancient sun god with parades, music, and dances that bring the city to life.

La Paz, Bolivia, is another fascinating city in the Andes, known for its dramatic setting and unique culture. Sitting at an altitude of around 12,000 feet, La Paz is one of the highest capital cities in the world. The city is nestled in a deep valley surrounded by mountains, with the snow-capped peak of Illimani visible in the distance. La Paz is a lively place filled with bustling markets, vibrant neighborhoods, and a mix of modern and traditional lifestyles. One of the most interesting places to visit in La Paz is the Witches' Market, where vendors sell herbs, amulets, and other items used in traditional Andean rituals. Here, visitors can find everything from dried llama fetuses to colorful powders believed to bring good luck. La Paz also has an incredible cable car system, called Mi Teleférico, which offers breathtaking views of the city and the surrounding mountains as it transports passengers across the valley. In La Paz, travelers can immerse themselves in Bolivian culture, enjoy traditional foods like salteñas (a type of empanada), and explore the nearby Valle de la Luna (Valley of the Moon), a surreal landscape of eroded rock formations just outside the city.

Quito, Ecuador, is another famous city nestled in the Andes and is known as the "City in the Sky." At nearly 9,350 feet above sea level, Quito is one of the highest capitals in the world. Quito has a rich history dating back to pre-Columbian times when it was an important Indigenous settlement, and it later became a Spanish colonial city in the 16th century. The historic center of Quito is a UNESCO World Heritage site and is famous for its well-preserved colonial architecture, cobblestone streets, and beautiful churches. Visitors to Quito can explore landmarks like the Church of San Francisco, which is one of the oldest churches in South America, and the Basilica del Voto Nacional, a massive Gothic-style basilica with stunning views of the city. Another unique attraction in Quito is the Mitad del Mundo, or "Middle of the World," where visitors can stand on the equator, with one foot in each hemisphere. Quito is also known for its vibrant culture, delicious food, and colorful festivals, like the annual Fiesta de la Mama Negra, which celebrates Indigenous and Spanish traditions with parades, music, and dancing.

Bogotá, Colombia, is another major city located in the Andes, and it's a place where modern life meets ancient history. At an altitude of about 8,660 feet, Bogotá is the capital of Colombia and one of the largest cities in South America. The city is known for its vibrant arts scene, bustling markets, and friendly people. Bogotá's historic district, La Candelaria, is filled with colorful colonial buildings, museums, and cafes, making it a popular destination for tourists. One of the most famous landmarks in Bogotá is the Gold Museum, which houses an impressive collection of pre-Columbian gold artifacts created by Indigenous peoples of the Andes. Bogotá is also known for its street art, with many murals that reflect the city's culture and history. Mount Monserrate, which rises over the city, offers incredible views and is a popular spot for both locals and visitors. A cable car takes people up to the top, where there's a beautiful church and small restaurants serving traditional Colombian dishes like ajiaco, a hearty chicken and potato soup. Bogotá's high-altitude setting gives it a cool climate, and the city's parks, plazas, and cultural events make it a lively and exciting place to visit.

Santiago, Chile, is a modern city with a stunning view of the Andes. Although Santiago is not as high in the mountains as other cities, the Andes form a dramatic backdrop that can be seen from almost anywhere in the city. Santiago is the capital and largest city of Chile, and it's a place where traditional culture meets urban life. Visitors can explore historic neighborhoods like Bellavista, known for its colorful street art and vibrant nightlife, or visit the central market, where fresh seafood and Chilean dishes are served. Santiago is also home to several impressive museums, such as the Museum of Pre-Columbian Art, which offers a look into the history and culture of Indigenous peoples from Chile and other parts of Latin America. For a view of the city and the surrounding mountains, visitors can take a funicular up to the top of Cerro San Cristóbal, a hill in the middle of Santiago that offers a panoramic view of the skyline and the Andes.

Santiago's location makes it easy to reach outdoor adventures, from skiing in the Andes during the winter months to wine tasting in the nearby vineyards of the Central Valley.

Mendoza, Argentina, is a city in the foothills of the Andes and is famous for its wine, particularly Malbec. Located in the heart of Argentina's wine country, Mendoza is surrounded by vineyards, with the Andes Mountains providing a stunning backdrop. The city has a sunny, dry climate that is ideal for grape-growing, and many wineries in the area offer tours and tastings. Mendoza is a popular destination for food and wine lovers, as well as for outdoor enthusiasts. The nearby Andes offer opportunities for hiking, rafting, and even mountaineering, with Aconcagua, the highest peak in the Andes, located just a short drive from the city. Mendoza's tree-lined streets, plazas, and relaxed atmosphere make it a charming place to visit, and its proximity to the mountains makes it a base for exploring the natural beauty of the Andes. Each year, the city celebrates the Fiesta Nacional de la Vendimia, or National Grape Harvest Festival, which includes parades, music, and traditional dances to celebrate the grape harvest and Mendoza's winemaking heritage.

Arequipa, Peru, is another beautiful Andean city known as the "White City" because of its stunning colonial buildings made from sillar, a white volcanic stone. Arequipa is surrounded by volcanoes, including the towering Misti Volcano, which is a popular spot for adventurous hikers. The city has a unique blend of Spanish and Indigenous culture, and its historic center is a UNESCO World Heritage site. Arequipa's Plaza de Armas is one of the most beautiful in Peru, surrounded by colonial buildings with elegant arches and the stunning Arequipa Cathedral. The city is also famous for its cuisine, with dishes like rocoto relleno (stuffed spicy peppers) and chupe de camarones (shrimp chowder) that reflect the region's culinary traditions. Arequipa's blend of history, culture, and natural beauty makes it a fascinating place to explore, and its location in the Andes means visitors can experience both the city's charm and the nearby mountains.

These cities in the Andes each offer a unique experience and a chance to connect with the rich culture, history, and natural beauty of the Andean region. Whether it's exploring ancient ruins in Cusco, shopping in the markets of La Paz, or tasting wine in Mendoza, visitors to these cities can discover the many different ways that life in the Andes is influenced by the mountains. From colorful festivals to architectural wonders and stunning landscapes, the cities of the Andes are full of surprises, making each one a memorable destination for anyone who visits.

Chapter 18: Unique Foods and Flavors of the Andes

The Andes Mountains are not only a place of stunning landscapes and rich history but also home to an extraordinary variety of foods and flavors. Andean cuisine is unique and full of surprises, shaped by thousands of years of Indigenous culture, Spanish colonial influence, and the diversity of ingredients found across this vast mountain range. The high altitudes, diverse climates, and fertile soils make the Andes a perfect place for growing unique foods that aren't found anywhere else in the world. From colorful potatoes and corn varieties to quinoa and exotic fruits, Andean cuisine is a reflection of the region's natural abundance and creativity. Many traditional Andean foods have been enjoyed for centuries, passed down through generations and adapted to suit local tastes. Let's dive into some of the unique ingredients and dishes that make the food of the Andes so special.

One of the most famous and ancient Andean foods is the potato. Potatoes were first domesticated in the Andes around 8,000 years ago, and the region is home to thousands of different varieties. Potatoes come in an incredible range of colors, shapes, and flavors—some are purple, others are red, yellow, or even blue. Each variety has its own taste and texture, making potatoes one of the most versatile ingredients in Andean cooking. In many Andean countries, there is a saying that a different type of potato can be eaten every day of the year without repeating. Some potatoes are soft and buttery, perfect for making mashed potatoes, while others are waxy and hold their shape in stews. A popular Andean dish called "papa a la huancaína" is made from boiled potatoes topped with a creamy sauce made of cheese, yellow peppers, and spices. Another common way to enjoy potatoes in the Andes is "chuño," a freeze-dried potato that has been preserved using a traditional technique. Chuño is made by leaving potatoes out overnight in the cold mountain air, then stepping on them to remove the moisture. This process gives the potatoes a unique texture and taste, and they can be stored for years, providing a reliable food source in times of scarcity.

Corn, or "maíz," is another essential ingredient in Andean cuisine, and like potatoes, it has been grown in the Andes for thousands of years. Andean corn is different from the sweet corn often found in North American diets; it comes in a variety of colors, including yellow, purple, and white, and has large, starchy kernels that are often chewy. One of the most popular types of Andean corn is "choclo," a large-kernel variety that is often served as a side dish or snack, grilled or boiled and sprinkled with salt. Corn is also used to make a traditional drink called "chicha," which has been enjoyed in the Andes since ancient times. Chicha is made by fermenting corn and sometimes flavored with fruits or spices. In some regions, chicha is still prepared in a traditional way, where the corn is chewed before fermenting, as enzymes in saliva help to break down the starch. This drink is usually enjoyed during festivals, ceremonies, and family gatherings, and it has a mildly alcoholic flavor. Corn is also used to make a popular Andean snack called "cancha," which is similar to roasted corn or popcorn. The large corn kernels are toasted until they're crunchy, then salted and enjoyed as a light snack.

Another important Andean food is quinoa, a grain that has gained worldwide popularity in recent years for its high nutritional value. Quinoa is a superfood packed with protein, fiber, and essential amino acids, making it an excellent choice for people who need energy and nourishment, especially in the harsh conditions of the high Andes. Quinoa has been cultivated in the Andes for over 5,000 years and was considered a sacred crop by the Incas, who called it the "mother grain." Quinoa is highly versatile and can be used in soups, salads, stews, and even desserts. In the Andes, quinoa is often cooked with vegetables and herbs to make a hearty stew or added to soups to give them a rich, nutty flavor. Quinoa comes in several colors, including white, red, and black, each with a slightly different taste and texture. Red quinoa is often used in salads for its firm texture, while white quinoa is softer and commonly used in soups and porridge. Quinoa has also become a symbol of pride in Andean culture, as it is a native crop that has brought international attention to the region's traditional foods.

The Andes are also known for their unique fruits, which are both delicious and unusual to people who live outside the region. One of these is the "lucuma," a fruit with green skin and bright orange flesh. Lucuma has a sweet, creamy taste that some people describe as a mix between maple and sweet potato. It is often used in desserts like ice cream, cakes, and smoothies, and it's popular in Peru, where locals use it to make lucuma-flavored treats. Another unique fruit is the "cherimoya," sometimes called the "custard apple" because of its creamy texture and sweet flavor. Cherimoya has a taste that's often described as a mix of banana, pineapple, and strawberry, and it's so beloved in the Andes that even Mark Twain once called it "the most delicious fruit known to men." Cherimoya is often eaten fresh, scooped out with a spoon, or added to fruit salads and desserts. Other unique Andean fruits include "aguaymanto" (also known as goldenberry or physalis), a small, yellow fruit that is both sweet and tangy, and "pepino," a melon-like fruit with a mild, refreshing flavor. These fruits not only add flavor to Andean cuisine but are also packed with vitamins and nutrients that help people stay healthy in the high-altitude environment.

In addition to these plant-based foods, Andean cuisine also includes unique types of meat. One of the most traditional meats in the Andes is "cuy," or guinea pig. While this might sound unusual to people outside the region, cuy has been a staple food in the Andes for centuries and is often prepared on special occasions. It's usually roasted or grilled, and the meat is said to have a flavor similar to rabbit or dark chicken meat. Cuy is high in protein and low in fat, making it a nutritious option for people living in the mountains. In some parts of the Andes, alpaca meat is also commonly eaten. Alpacas are domesticated animals related to llamas, and their meat is tender, lean, and slightly sweet. Alpaca meat is often grilled, stewed, or used in sausages, and it's prized for its high protein content and low fat. Both cuy and alpaca are examples of how Andean people use the resources available to them to create nourishing meals that fit their environment and lifestyle.

Spices and herbs play a crucial role in Andean cooking as well, adding depth and complexity to the dishes. "Ají," a type of chili pepper, is one of the most commonly used spices in Andean cuisine, and it comes in many varieties, each with its own level of heat and flavor. Ají amarillo, or yellow chili, is a popular choice that adds a bright, fruity flavor and a vibrant yellow color to sauces, stews, and marinades. One famous Andean sauce made from ají amarillo is "ají de gallina," a creamy, spicy chicken dish that's often served with rice and potatoes. Another commonly used herb is "huacatay," also known as Peruvian black mint. Huacatay has a unique flavor that is slightly minty, with hints of basil and anise, and it's often used to flavor sauces and meats. One popular sauce made from huacatay is "ocopa," a rich, creamy sauce typically served over potatoes.

The Andes are also known for their refreshing beverages made from local ingredients. Aside from chicha, one popular drink is "mate de coca," a tea made from coca leaves. Coca leaves have been used by Indigenous Andean people for centuries, as they contain natural compounds that help reduce the symptoms of altitude sickness, like fatigue and shortness of breath. Drinking mate de coca is a common way to adapt to the high altitudes of the Andes, and it's often served to visitors to help them adjust. Another popular Andean drink is "emoliente," a warm herbal tea made from a mix of medicinal plants, such as barley, flaxseed, and aloe vera. Emoliente is especially popular in the cool Andean evenings, and it's believed to have health benefits that soothe the stomach and boost energy.

The foods of the Andes are deeply connected to the land and the people who live there. Each ingredient, whether it's a colorful potato, a tangy fruit, or a spicy pepper, reflects the resourcefulness and creativity of Andean cultures. Through their unique foods, the people of the Andes have created a cuisine that is as rich and varied as the landscapes they inhabit. Andean food isn't just about nourishment—it's a celebration of nature, history, and culture, and every meal tells a story of the mountains, the valleys, and the traditions that have been passed down through generations.

Chapter 19: Protecting the Andes Environment

The Andes Mountains are one of the world's most important and unique ecosystems, stretching over 4,300 miles along the western side of South America and providing a home to countless species of plants, animals, and communities of people. But despite its beauty and natural richness, the Andes are facing serious environmental challenges that threaten the balance of life in this vast mountain range. Protecting the Andes environment is crucial, not only for the people and wildlife that live there but also for the health of our planet. The Andes provide essential resources, such as fresh water, which flows down from glaciers and rivers to supply cities, farms, and communities. They also have huge areas of forests that help to absorb carbon dioxide, playing a role in slowing down climate change. However, rising temperatures, deforestation, mining, and pollution are putting tremendous pressure on these resources, and finding ways to protect the Andes is more important than ever.

One of the biggest environmental challenges in the Andes is climate change, which is having a noticeable impact on this region, especially at high altitudes. The Andes have thousands of glaciers, which are like nature's water towers, storing and slowly releasing water into rivers that flow down to towns and villages below. This glacier water is essential for drinking, farming, and hydropower (electricity generated from water) in countries like Peru, Bolivia, and Ecuador. However, due to rising temperatures, these glaciers are melting much faster than they used to. Some of the smaller glaciers have already disappeared, while others are retreating, shrinking in size every year. If these glaciers continue to melt, people and wildlife who depend on them for water could face serious shortages. For example, in the dry season, when there's less rainfall, glacier meltwater is especially important for crops, animals, and people. Without it, farmers might not have enough water for their fields, and the rivers could run low, affecting fish and other animals that depend on this water source. Protecting glaciers is a complex challenge because it requires global efforts to reduce carbon emissions and slow down climate change, but local communities in the Andes are also taking steps to adapt by finding new ways to conserve and manage water more efficiently.

Deforestation is another serious threat to the Andes environment. Forests are incredibly valuable to the Andes because they help to maintain healthy soil, store carbon, and provide habitat for animals. However, many Andean forests, especially the cloud forests, are being cut down to make way for farms, roads, and cities. Cloud forests, which are named for the mist and clouds that surround them, are found in the lower parts of the Andes and are home to unique plants and animals that can't live anywhere else. When these forests are cut down, not only do animals lose their homes, but the land also becomes more vulnerable to erosion. Erosion is when soil is washed away by rain or wind, making the ground less stable and harder for new plants to grow. In some areas, landslides become more common when forests are cleared, posing a danger to people living nearby. Trees in Andean forests also play an important role in trapping carbon dioxide, one of the main greenhouse gases that cause global warming. When forests are cut down, the carbon stored in those trees is released back into the atmosphere, which contributes to climate change. Protecting Andean forests is essential, and many organizations and governments are working to create protected areas and promote sustainable farming practices that reduce the need for deforestation.

Mining is another major environmental issue in the Andes. The mountains are rich in valuable minerals like gold, copper, and silver, and mining has been a big part of the economy in Andean countries for hundreds of years. While mining provides jobs and resources, it also has a significant impact on the environment. Mining activities can pollute rivers and soil with toxic chemicals, such as mercury and cyanide, which are used to extract metals from rocks. These chemicals can be harmful to fish, plants, and people who rely on clean water. When mining companies dig large pits or build tunnels, they also disrupt the landscape, making it difficult for plants and animals to survive in those areas. In some cases, entire mountainsides are stripped of vegetation, leaving behind bare, rocky land. Many Andean communities are concerned about the impact of mining on their water sources, as polluted water can flow downstream, affecting farms, animals, and drinking supplies far from the mining site. In response, some countries in the Andes are working to enforce stricter environmental regulations for mining companies, and communities are advocating for cleaner and more sustainable mining practices.

Agriculture is another factor affecting the Andes environment. Farming has always been an important part of life in the Andes, with Indigenous communities creating complex systems like terraces to grow crops on the steep mountain slopes. However, as populations grow and demand for food increases, some farming practices are putting pressure on the land and water resources. Modern agriculture often relies on chemicals like fertilizers and pesticides to increase crop yields, but these chemicals can pollute rivers and harm wildlife. In addition, large-scale farming sometimes leads to soil erosion, especially when forests are cleared to create new fields. Traditional farming practices, such as terrace farming, are more sustainable because they prevent soil erosion and conserve water, but they take more time and labor. Some environmental organizations are encouraging farmers in the Andes to use traditional methods and organic farming techniques to reduce the impact on the environment. By balancing modern needs with traditional wisdom, it's possible to protect the land while still growing enough food for local communities.

Wildlife conservation is also a crucial part of protecting the Andes environment. The Andes are home to an astonishing variety of animals, many of which are found nowhere else on Earth. These include iconic species like the Andean condor, the largest flying bird in the world, and the spectacled bear, which is the only bear species native to South America. However, habitat loss, hunting, and climate change are threatening the survival of many Andean animals. For example, as glaciers melt and temperatures rise, the habitats of certain species, like the Andean flamingo and the mountain tapir, are shrinking, putting them at risk. Conservation efforts are underway to protect these animals and their habitats. National parks and nature reserves have been established in many parts of the Andes to provide safe spaces for wildlife. Some organizations are also working with local communities to raise awareness about the importance of protecting animals and to discourage hunting of endangered species. By involving people who live in the Andes in conservation efforts, these programs help to create a sense of responsibility and respect for the environment.

Water conservation is another key issue in the Andes, especially as climate change affects water availability. In some parts of the Andes, water is already a scarce resource, and it becomes even more precious as glaciers melt and rainfall patterns change. Many Andean communities rely on traditional water management systems, such as canals and reservoirs, which were built by the Incas and other Indigenous cultures to store and distribute water. These systems help to capture rainwater during the wet season and store it for use during the dry season, ensuring that there's enough water for crops, animals, and people. Today, some communities are reviving these ancient techniques to adapt to modern water challenges. In addition, new technologies like drip irrigation, which delivers water directly to the roots of plants, are being introduced to help farmers use water more efficiently. Protecting the water resources of the Andes is not only important for the people who live there but also for the plants and animals that depend on clean, flowing rivers to survive.

Finally, ecotourism is playing an important role in protecting the Andes environment. Ecotourism is a type of tourism that focuses on experiencing nature in a way that respects and preserves the environment. In the Andes, ecotourism allows visitors to enjoy the stunning landscapes, hike along ancient trails, and observe unique wildlife, all while supporting conservation efforts. Ecotourism can provide income for local communities and encourage them to protect their natural resources. For example, in places like Peru's Sacred Valley, eco-lodges and guided tours help create jobs and generate income, while also raising awareness about the importance of protecting the environment. Many ecotourism businesses are committed to minimizing their impact on the land, using renewable energy, and supporting local conservation projects. By choosing eco-friendly tourism options, visitors can help to protect the Andes and ensure that future generations can continue to experience its natural beauty.

Protecting the Andes environment is a complex and ongoing challenge that requires the cooperation of governments, communities, and individuals. The Andes provide essential resources, like water and clean air, that benefit not only the people and wildlife who live there but also the entire world. By conserving forests, protecting wildlife, managing water wisely, and reducing pollution from mining and agriculture, it's possible to preserve the Andes for future generations. Through education, sustainable practices, and respect for traditional knowledge, people in the Andes and around the world can work together to protect this incredible mountain range, ensuring that its ecosystems remain healthy and vibrant for years to come. The Andes are a treasure trove of biodiversity and natural wonders, and by taking steps to protect them, we are not only helping the environment but also preserving a vital part of our global heritage.

Chapter 20: The Future of the Andes Mountains

The Andes Mountains are one of the world's most remarkable natural wonders, stretching across seven countries in South America and holding a vast array of unique landscapes, diverse wildlife, and ancient cultures. But as we look to the future, many questions arise about what lies ahead for this magnificent mountain range. The future of the Andes is deeply connected to how humans interact with the environment, respond to climate change, protect resources, and balance progress with conservation. Many challenges threaten the Andes today, from rising temperatures and melting glaciers to deforestation and pollution. However, with innovative ideas, scientific research, and the efforts of local communities, there is hope for a future where the Andes continue to thrive. Exploring what might happen to the Andes Mountains in the future helps us understand the importance of acting now to protect these majestic peaks for generations to come.

One of the most pressing issues for the future of the Andes is climate change, which is affecting the region at an alarming rate. The Andes have thousands of glaciers that are not only beautiful but also provide crucial water supplies for millions of people, especially during dry seasons when rivers and rain alone aren't enough. These glaciers are like nature's water reservoirs, slowly releasing water into rivers that flow down to cities and farms. But as global temperatures rise, these glaciers are melting faster than they can be replaced. Some scientists predict that if the current rate of warming continues, many glaciers in the Andes could disappear within the next few decades. This would mean severe water shortages for communities, less water for crops, and even reduced electricity from hydropower plants, which rely on flowing water to generate energy. People in the Andes are already feeling the effects, with rivers running lower and water becoming scarcer during the dry season. The future of the Andes depends on finding ways to slow down this glacier loss, which could involve global efforts to reduce greenhouse gas emissions, along with local efforts to conserve water and find alternative sources.

Another critical aspect of the Andes' future is the need to preserve its unique ecosystems, especially the cloud forests, grasslands, and páramo (high-altitude moorlands). These ecosystems support a huge diversity of plants and animals, many of which are found nowhere else on Earth. However, human activities like farming, logging, and urban expansion are shrinking these habitats, putting wildlife at risk. For example, the Andean condor, spectacled bear, and mountain tapir are just a few of the species that rely on these unique habitats to survive. As more land is cleared for agriculture or development, these animals are losing their homes and, in some cases, are being driven closer to extinction. In the future, there may be even greater pressure on these lands as the population grows and the demand for farmland increases. But there's hope in the efforts of conservation organizations, governments, and local communities who are working to protect and restore these areas. Programs to create national parks, nature reserves, and protected areas are vital, as they provide safe spaces where wildlife can thrive. In addition, sustainable farming practices and reforestation projects help restore damaged areas and give ecosystems a chance to recover. Protecting these ecosystems is not just about saving wildlife; it's also about preserving the health of the Andes as a whole, as these areas help regulate water cycles, store carbon, and support the people who live nearby.

Deforestation is one of the biggest challenges facing the Andes' future. Forests, particularly in the cloud forest regions, play a huge role in absorbing carbon dioxide from the atmosphere, which helps reduce the effects of climate change. Unfortunately, many of these forests are being cut down to make room for agriculture, mining, and urban development. The loss of these trees means not only that more carbon is released into the atmosphere but also that the soil is more likely to erode, rivers are at risk of drying up, and biodiversity suffers. In recent years, there has been a growing movement to protect Andean forests and promote reforestation efforts. Communities, governments, and environmental organizations are working to plant trees, restore forests, and promote sustainable practices that reduce the need for deforestation. Looking ahead, the success of these efforts could play a major role in the future of the Andes. By protecting forests and replanting trees, we can help reduce the impact of climate change, preserve water resources, and provide a healthy habitat for countless species.

Water scarcity is another pressing issue that will shape the Andes' future. As glaciers melt and rainfall patterns change due to climate change, water resources in the Andes are becoming less reliable. This is a huge concern because so many people in the Andes, especially in rural areas, rely on rivers, streams, and underground sources for their water needs. The future will likely bring an increased focus on finding ways to conserve water and manage it more efficiently. In some places, ancient water management techniques developed by the Inca and other Indigenous cultures are being revived to help adapt to these changes. These include building terraces, canals, and reservoirs that store water and prevent it from running off too quickly. Modern technology can also help, such as drip irrigation, which reduces the amount of water needed for farming by delivering it directly to the roots of plants. Local communities, scientists, and governments are working together to create strategies that balance the needs of agriculture, cities, and nature. By planning for the future and making careful decisions about water use, it may be possible to ensure that the Andes continue to provide for the people who live there.

The future of the Andes is also connected to sustainable economic development. The Andes contain valuable minerals like gold, silver, and copper, which have been mined for centuries and are a major part of the economy in many Andean countries. However, mining can be very harmful to the environment, as it often leads to pollution of rivers and soil, destruction of natural landscapes, and health risks for local communities. In recent years, there has been a push for more responsible mining practices that minimize environmental damage and provide benefits to local communities. Some mining companies are adopting stricter environmental standards and using cleaner technologies, while others are working with local communities to create fair partnerships. There are also efforts to diversify the economy, focusing on activities that are less damaging to the environment, such as ecotourism. Ecotourism allows people to experience the beauty of the Andes while supporting conservation efforts, as many ecotourism projects use their profits to fund environmental protection and community development. In the future, sustainable tourism could play an even bigger role in the Andes, providing income and jobs without harming the natural resources.

Cultural preservation is another important factor in the future of the Andes. Indigenous peoples, such as the Quechua and Aymara, have lived in the Andes for thousands of years and have deep cultural and spiritual connections to the land. However, as modernization and urbanization continue, there is a risk that some of these traditions and ways of life could be lost. Preserving the cultural heritage of the Andes is not only about honoring history but also about protecting knowledge and practices that can help solve modern problems. Many traditional Andean practices, such as terrace farming, medicinal plant use, and communal resource management, offer sustainable solutions to environmental and social challenges. In the future, efforts to protect and celebrate Andean cultures will be key to maintaining a strong sense of identity and connection to the land. Governments, schools, and cultural organizations are working to support Indigenous languages, arts, and customs, recognizing that these are valuable parts of the Andes' heritage.

Innovation and technology also have an important role to play in the future of the Andes. Scientists and researchers are studying the Andes to understand more about climate change, biodiversity, and ancient civilizations. This research helps us learn how to protect the Andes and adapt to changes in the environment. For example, scientists are using satellite technology to monitor glacier melting and deforestation, which helps create better conservation strategies. Renewable energy technologies, such as solar and wind power, are also being explored as sustainable energy sources for Andean communities. In many rural areas, people still rely on wood for cooking and heating, which can lead to deforestation. By using renewable energy, it's possible to reduce the pressure on forests and provide a cleaner, more reliable energy source for people in the Andes. Additionally, educational programs are helping young people learn about environmental science, sustainable practices, and new technologies, so they can play a role in protecting their homeland as future leaders.

In the future, international cooperation will be essential to protect the Andes. The Andes Mountains stretch across multiple countries, including Venezuela, Colombia, Ecuador, Peru, Bolivia, Chile, and Argentina. Environmental issues like climate change, water management, and deforestation don't stop at national borders, so countries in the Andes must work together to create solutions. Many organizations and governments are already collaborating on conservation projects, scientific research, and environmental policies that benefit the region as a whole. For example, countries in the Andes have joined forces to create a network of protected areas and share resources for conservation projects. By continuing to work together, these nations can create stronger, more effective plans to protect the Andes and ensure a sustainable future.

The future of the Andes Mountains is filled with both challenges and opportunities. This unique and precious environment faces serious threats from climate change, deforestation, and human activity, but there is also hope in the efforts of people who are working to protect it. From local communities and scientists to governments and international organizations, many groups are joining forces to find solutions that will help the Andes thrive. Protecting the Andes requires a combination of traditional knowledge and modern science, sustainable practices, and a commitment to preserving the culture and biodiversity that make this region so special. By taking action today, we can help create a future where the Andes remain a place of wonder, beauty, and life for generations to come.

Epilogue

You've reached the end of our journey through the Andes Mountains! Along the way, we explored towering peaks, ancient ruins, rare wildlife, and unique cultures. We learned how the Andes were formed, discovered the challenges of life at high altitudes, and uncovered the secrets hidden within misty cloud forests and vibrant valleys. The Andes are more than just a mountain range; they're a place of wonder, where history, nature, and adventure meet.

The story of the Andes doesn't stop here. Every day, scientists, explorers, and local communities continue to learn more about this incredible region. They work together to protect the delicate balance of life in these mountains and to preserve the cultures and traditions that make the Andes unique. With climate change and new challenges facing the natural world, the Andes need people who care and want to help protect their future.

As you close this book, remember that the Andes are out there, continuing to inspire and amaze. Who knows? Maybe one day you'll be one of the people who explores, studies, or helps protect these magnificent mountains. Until then, keep your curiosity alive and your sense of adventure strong—because the world is full of incredible places just waiting to be discovered. The Andes will be here, ready for you, whenever you're ready for the next adventure.

The End.

Milton Keynes UK
Ingram Content Group UK Ltd.
UKHW041938241124
451423UK00001BA/194